# Personal Independence Payment

## What you need to know

Child Poverty Action Group

Published by Child Poverty Action Group
30 Micawber Street
London N1 7TB
Tel: 020 7837 7979
staff@cpag.org.uk
cpag.org.uk

A CIP record for this book is available from the British Library.
ISBN: 978 1 915324 18 4

Child Poverty Action Group is a charity registered in England and Wales (registration number 294841) and in Scotland (registration number SC039339), and is a company limited by guarantee, registered in England (registration number 1993854). VAT number: 690 808117

Internal design by Devious Designs
Cover design by Colorido Studios
Typeset by DLxml, a division of RefineCatch Limited, Bungay, Suffolk
Content management system by KonnectSoft
Printed and bound in the UK by CPI Group (UK) Ltd

**Author**
**Harriet Chaplin** is a welfare rights adviser at CPAG.

**Acknowledgements**
Thanks are due to the authors of the previous editions. Many thanks to Carri Swann for her valuable comments for this edition. Thanks also to Pauline Phillips for editing and managing the production, Anne Ketley for compiling the index and Kathleen Armstrong for proofreading the text.

## About Child Poverty Action Group

We provide trusted and expert information and advice for the welfare rights and advice community – online, and through our books, training and advice services. Our advice lines support thousands of advisers a year, helping them to give families the best information and advice. Our *Welfare Benefits Handbook*, described as the 'adviser's bible', is used by Citizens Advice, local authorities and law centres throughout the UK. We also keep advisers up to date with trends and changes in the social security system through bulletins and our highly regarded training courses and seminars.

Poverty affects one in four children in the UK today. When children grow up poor they miss out – and so do the rest of us. They miss out on the things most children take for granted: warm clothes, school trips, having friends over for tea. They do less well at school and earn less as adults. Any family can fall on hard times and find it difficult to make ends meet. But poverty is not inevitable. With the right policies every child can have the opportunity to do well in life, and we all share the rewards of having a stronger economy and a healthier, fairer society.

If you would like to join us to help end child poverty, please visit cpag.org.uk or follow us on Facebook (facebook.com/cpaguk) and X (@cpaguk).

### Keeping up to date

Advisers can get the latest information on personal independence payment by booking on a CPAG training course. We can also provide your workplace with in-house training. See cpag.org.uk/training for more information.

Our *Welfare Benefits Handbook*, published every April, tells you all you need to know about entitlement to benefits and other payments, and contains the latest information on appeals. With up-to-date information, insights, decision-making tools and appeal letter generators, CPAG Welfare Rights is our online platform that supplements the expertise advisers have come to trust and rely on from our rights handbooks and training. CPAG Welfare Rights provides digital access to our flagship *Welfare Benefits Handbook*, which is fully searchable and updated throughout the year online. See cpag.org.uk/subscriptions to subscribe or find out more.

## Getting advice

Your local Citizens Advice or other advice centre can give you advice and support on benefits. See citizensadvice.org.uk if you live in England or Wales, or cas.org.uk if you live in Scotland.

CPAG has an advice line for advisers. If you can't hear or speak on the phone, you can contact the advice line using Relay UK.

For advisers in the UK:
Telephone: 020 7812 5231, Monday to Friday 10am to 12pm and 2pm to 4pm

For advisers in Scotland:
Telephone: 0141 552 0552, Monday to Thursday 10am to 4pm and Friday 10am to 12pm
Email: advice@cpagscotland.org.uk

# Contents

## Note

Terms put in 'quotation marks', the first time they are used in a section, are defined in either Appendix 1 (except in a few cases where they are explained in that same section) or Appendix 2 (for terms used in the 'descriptors').

Throughout the book, the Department for Work and Pensions is referred to as the DWP.

# Chapter 1
# Introduction

This chapter covers:

1. What is personal independence payment?
2. Personal independence payment and disability living allowance
3. What does this guide cover?

## What you need to know

- Personal independence payment (PIP) is a benefit paid to disabled adults who have difficulty with day-to-day tasks, moving around or going out. It is paid by the Department for Work and Pensions (DWP).
- It has two 'components': daily living and mobility. Each is paid at a standard or enhanced rate. You can qualify for one or both components.
- PIP is not means tested. This means any income or capital you have does not affect your entitlement to PIP. You can get PIP if you are in or out of work.
- You usually initially claim PIP by phone, then complete a questionnaire and attend an assessment with a 'healthcare professional'.
- You are assessed on how your health or disability affects your ability to carry out 12 everyday activities.
- You are normally awarded PIP for a fixed period and then reassessed.
- If you are refused PIP, you can first ask for the decision to be reconsidered and then appeal to a tribunal if needed.

- You can only claim PIP in England, Wales and Northern Ireland. In Scotland, the equivalent benefit is adult disability payment.

## 1. What is personal independence payment?

PIP is a benefit for working-age people (usually aged 16 to state pension age) with an illness or disability that affects their ability to complete daily tasks. The person must have had their difficulties for at least three months, and expect the difficulties to last for the next nine months.

It was introduced for new claimants in Great Britain in 2013. It was introduced in June 2016 in Northern Ireland. This book explains the rules in Great Britain. You cannot make a new claim for PIP if you live in Scotland. Those living in Scotland who still receive PIP will be transferred to adult disability payment. The Scottish government aims to complete this by the end of 2025, though this may change. There is more information about adult disability payment in CPAG's *Welfare Benefits Handbook*.

PIP replaced adult disability living allowance. Those who still receive disability living allowance were being transferred to PIP; however, this process has been suspended since November 2022. If you are receiving disability living allowance, you can still choose to make a claim for PIP; however, you should get free benefits advice before doing so.

The DWP administers and pays PIP. It is not 'means tested' and you can receive it whether you are in or out of work. You do not have to have made any national insurance contributions to qualify and PIP is not taxable. It is paid on top of most other benefits.

PIP is made up of two 'components': a 'daily living component', paid if you have difficulty carrying out specified daily living activities, and a 'mobility component', paid if you have difficulty going out or moving around. You may qualify for one or both components. Each component is paid at a standard and an enhanced (higher) rate.

Entitlement to the different components and rates of PIP can also qualify you and your carer for other benefits and schemes, including carer's allowance, a blue badge for parking, exemption from road tax and help from the Motability scheme.

Although PIP is designed to help with the extra costs of ill health or disability, you can use the money in any way you wish and do not have to account for how you spend it.

**How are you assessed and paid?**

You usually make a claim for PIP by phone. You must then usually fill in a questionnaire about how your health or disability affects you, and attend a consultation with a 'healthcare professional' who assesses your difficulties. The healthcare professional sends a report to the DWP, where a 'case manager' decides whether you qualify for PIP.

To qualify, you must show that your ability to carry out a range of everyday activities is limited because of your physical or mental condition. There are 10 daily living activities and two mobility activities. Each activity is described by a number of statements (called 'descriptors') which reflect different levels of ability. Each descriptor is given a score; the greater the level of difficulty described, the higher the score. You only score points for one descriptor within each activity. The DWP decides which descriptors you satisfy. You must score at least eight points in total to qualify for the standard rate of the daily living or mobility component. If you score 12 points or more, you qualify for the enhanced rate.

Awards of PIP are usually made for a fixed period. You are paid into your bank account, usually every four weeks. You can be reassessed at any time, although this normally happens when your award is coming to an end, when you report a change in your condition, or if the DWP thinks your case should be reviewed. Shorter awards are not automatically renewed. If you haven't heard from the DWP six months before your award is due to end, you should contact the DWP to check whether you need to make a new claim.

If you are refused PIP, or receive less money than you think you should get, you can ask for the decision to be reconsidered by the DWP and then appeal to an independent tribunal if needed.

Special rules apply if you have a 'terminal illness', or if you are in a care home, hospital or prison.

## 2. Personal independence payment and disability living allowance

PIP replaces adult disability living allowance for people of working age (aged 16 to state pension age). Most people will be asked to move from disability living allowance to PIP; however, at the time of writing this process was suspended. You can still get disability living allowance for children under 16, and attendance allowance if you are state pension age or over.

If you were under 65 on 8 April 2013 and still get disability living allowance, you will be asked to claim PIP at some point in the next few years.

If you are already getting child disability living allowance and you turn 16, the DWP will write to you telling you that you must claim PIP instead. The DWP usually does this around six months before you turn 16. Your disability living allowance ends when your PIP claim is decided. There are exceptions to this rule if you live in Scotland, have a 'terminal illness' or are in hospital when you turn 16. If you are terminally ill, you continue to receive disability living allowance regardless of age. If you are in hospital, you can continue to receive disability living allowance, but when you leave hospital or your disability living allowance award is due to run out, you can still be asked to claim PIP at that point. If you live in Scotland, you can continue to receive disability living allowance until you are 18, at which point you are invited to claim adult disability payment.

It is important to remember that even if you have an award of disability living allowance, you may not qualify for an award of PIP due to the difference in eligibility criteria. It may be helpful to gain specialist advice to talk you through which rate of PIP you may expect to receive in comparison to any existing disability living allowance awards.

The process of transferring adult disability living allowance claimants to PIP happens as follows.

- You will be sent a letter inviting you to claim PIP.
- The letter will give you a deadline to claim. This is 28 days from the date on the letter.
- If you do not claim PIP within this time limit, your disability living allowance will stop.
- This time limit can be extended if it is reasonable to do so.
- The stoppage of disability living allowance is a suspension, and disability living allowance can be reinstated for another 28 days if you then make a claim for PIP.
- If you fail to make a claim for PIP within this extended 28-day period, your disability living allowance will end.

If you receive disability living allowance, the process for claiming PIP is the same as for everyone, as described in Chapters 3, 4, 5 and 6.

If you do not want to claim PIP, you can tell the DWP this, and your disability living allowance award will end two weeks after your next payday.

If you currently receive disability living allowance, you have to claim PIP instead if either of the following applies.

- You report there has been a change in your condition that could affect your disability living allowance award, unless you are in hospital and still getting paid your disability living allowance or the change is that you go abroad.
- Your disability living allowance award is coming to an end.

Neither of the above bullet points apply if you are under 16 (under 18 in Scotland) or turned 65 before 8 April 2013.

You may decide by yourself to claim PIP and move from disability living allowance. It is important to be aware that once you start this process it cannot be stopped, meaning you cannot return to disability living allowance. Get advice before doing so if you are unsure.

## 3. What does this guide cover?

This guide covers the main aspects of PIP, including:

- who can claim and the main conditions you must meet to be entitled (Chapter 2)
- how to claim and how you are assessed (Chapter 3)
- details of the disability assessment criteria, including the 'activities' you are tested against and the points you must score to qualify for an award (Chapters 4, 5 and 6)
- how you can challenge decisions or qualify for a higher award if how your condition affects you changes (Chapter 7)
- how PIP is affected if you have a 'terminal illness' or are in hospital, a care home or prison (Chapter 8)
- how PIP can help you qualify for other benefits (Chapter 9)

Chapter 2

# Who can get personal independence payment

This chapter covers:

1. Who can get personal independence payment?
2. What are the rules about your age?
3. What are the nationality and residence rules?

**What you need to know**

- To receive an award of personal independence payment (PIP), your difficulties must relate to your physical or mental condition; however, this does not mean you require a specific diagnosis.
- To get PIP, you must be 16 or over.
- Normally, you cannot claim PIP for the first time if you are state pension age or over.
- If you are not a British citizen, or have recently spent time abroad, you may not be able to receive PIP.

## 1. Who can get personal independence payment?

You might be able to get PIP if you have a long-term health condition or a disability.

If you currently receive disability living allowance, it is important to receive free benefits advice before making a claim for PIP. This is because the qualifying criteria for PIP is very different. For example, the low rate 'care component' of disability living allowance does not have an equivalent in PIP.

You may lose your disability living allowance award if you choose to make a claim for PIP.

*What the law says*

**The basic rules of entitlement**

- To get PIP, you must meet conditions relating to your:
  - age
  - nationality
  - country of residence
  - health problems or disability
- PIP has a mobility component and a daily living component, each paid at a standard or enhanced rate depending on the difficulties you have with a set list of activities. To qualify for a component, you must have had your difficulties for at least three months and expect to have them for at least nine months more (unless you are 'terminally ill').

*Part 4 Welfare Reform Act 2012*

Chapters 4, 5 and 6 cover the rules on how the effects of your health condition or disability are assessed to see if you qualify for PIP.

Even if you qualify, PIP might not be paid to you if you are in prison, in hospital or in a care home. The rules about this are explained in Chapter 8.

You can qualify for PIP regardless of your income and savings, and whether or not you are working. You do not have to pay national insurance contributions to qualify.

## 2. What are the rules about your age?

You can claim PIP if you are between the ages of 16 and state pension age. In some cases, you can get PIP after you have reached state pension age.

To find out when you reach state pension age, visit gov.uk/state-pension-age.

You cannot get PIP until you are 16. If you are younger than 16, your parent or another adult can claim child disability living allowance on your behalf.

## Are you state pension age or older?

Normally, you must make a claim for PIP before you reach state pension age. If your health condition or disability starts to affect you after you turn state pension age, you are not entitled to PIP and must claim attendance allowance instead. If you already get attendance allowance, you cannot receive PIP.

If you claim PIP just before you reach state pension age and you meet the entitlement conditions, an award can be made to you, even if the decision on your claim is not made until after you reach state pension age.

If you already get PIP when you turn state pension age, your award normally has a set date on which it ends. You can renew your award by making a new claim in the months before it ends, but you must be claiming for the same disability or health problem, or a new condition that has developed from it. You can also claim PIP again if it is less than a year since your award ended, even though you are older than state pension age. Again, your claim must be based on the same condition or a new one that has developed from the condition. There are special rules about when you can get the 'mobility component' once you have reached state pension age (see below for more detail).

If you were under 65 on 8 April 2013, you are now state pension age or older, and you stopped getting disability living allowance less than a year ago, you can claim PIP no matter what your health condition is, provided you meet the normal rules of entitlement. The special rules about the mobility component described in the next section do not apply to you the first time you claim PIP.

If you were over 65 on 8 April 2013, you can continue receiving disability living allowance and will not be transferred to PIP. This means if you have a change in your circumstances, your disability living allowance will be reviewed rather than moving to PIP.

EXAMPLE

**65-year-olds**

Clarice has multiple sclerosis. She was first awarded PIP in March 2022. She then goes into remission and her award ends on 24 January 2023 after she reports the change in her circumstances. She reached state pension age on 31 May 2022.

By July 2023, Clarice's condition has worsened again. Although she is pension age, she can make a new claim for PIP as it is less than a year since her previous award ended. Clarice could also choose to claim attendance allowance. She gets advice at her local Citizens Advice and is told that it is better for her to claim PIP again as she could get the mobility component if she had qualified for it in her previous claim.

If you are getting PIP and you are now state pension age or older, you can ask for your award to be looked at again because your circumstances have changed. You can be awarded a different rate of the 'daily living component' and, if you were getting the mobility component, you can qualify for the daily living component for the first time even if you are state pension age or over. However, there are special rules that limit your entitlement to the mobility component once you are state pension age.

### How is your mobility component affected when you are state pension age?

You cannot qualify for the mobility component of PIP for the first time if your mobility is first affected after you reach state pension age.

If you are state pension age, and already get the mobility component, you can continue to receive it until your award ends. You can then make a renewal claim and continue to receive the same rate of the mobility component. Your mobility needs must arise from the same condition as your previous award or from a new condition that has developed from that condition.

If your needs have decreased, you may be awarded the standard rate rather than your previous enhanced rate.

If your needs have increased, your award cannot increase from the standard rate to the enhanced rate.

If the DWP changes your PIP award after you reach state pension age (for example, because your circumstances have changed or your original award was not correct), you are only awarded the mobility component if you currently get it, or you used to get it less than a year ago but it stopped. The same rules apply regarding decreasing or increasing the rate you are entitled to, as explained above.

EXAMPLE

**Mobility component for people state pension age and over**

Evangelina is 67. She has arthritis and gets the standard rate of PIP daily living component and the standard rate of the mobility component.

Evangelina is involved in a road traffic accident and is left paralysed from the waist down. She asks for her award to be looked at again.

Her daily living component award is changed to the enhanced rate, but Evangelina cannot be awarded the enhanced rate of the mobility component. She meets the normal entitlement conditions, but her mobility component award cannot be increased because the accident happened after she reached state pension age.

## 3. What are the nationality and residence rules?

The rules can prevent you from getting PIP if you are not a UK national or if you have recently spent time abroad. This is a complicated area of law and you are likely to need specialist benefit advice, which you can find at advicelocal.uk.

### Are you a foreign national?

If you are not a British or Irish national, you may be a 'person subject to immigration control'.

Most people who are subject to immigration control cannot claim PIP. If you are in any doubt about whether you are a person subject to immigration control, it is vital that you get specialist immigration advice before you make a claim for PIP. This is because making a claim when you are not allowed to do so can affect your right to stay in the UK.

If you have settled or pre-settled status under the 'European Union Settlement Scheme', you can claim PIP. However, the rules for people who have spent time abroad may mean you do not qualify.

There are complicated rules that may mean you can claim PIP if you have been helped to come to the UK by a friend or relative who is your sponsor. Get advice if this may apply to you, before you make a claim.

### Have you spent time abroad?

The rules on residence apply to everyone who claims PIP, even if you are a UK national.

There are a number of exceptions to the standard rules on residence.

- If you are 'terminally ill', you do not have to have been in Great Britain for two of the last three years.

- If you work in certain occupations, such as aircraft cabin crew, sailors or oil rig workers, time spent outside Great Britain for work can be ignored. You must be a UK employee for this rule to apply.
- If you or a member of your family you live with are serving abroad in the UK armed forces, the rules treat you as if you are in Great Britain.
- If you have refugee leave or humanitarian protection, you do not have to have been in Great Britain for two of the last three years.
- If you were living in Afghanistan, Ukraine, Sudan, Israel, Lebanon or the Occupied Palestinian Territories, and left in relation to the ongoing conflicts, you do not have to have been in Great Britain for two of the last three years.
- You are treated as if you are still in Great Britain during certain temporary absences.
- If you have spent time elsewhere in Europe, special European rules can help you to meet the standard tests using time spent living in another European country. You should get benefits advice.

*What the law says*

**Residence in Great Britain**

To get PIP you must normally:

- be present in Great Britain now
- have been present in Great Britain for two of the last three years
- be 'habitually resident' in the UK or Ireland (including the Isle of Man and the Channel Islands)

For more information about what 'habitually resident' means, see Box A below.

*Regulation 16 Social Security (Personal Independence Payment) Regulations 2013*

Box A

**What does 'habitually resident' mean?**

The meaning of 'habitual residence' has been defined by many court decisions over the years. You need to have had an 'appreciable period in the UK' and have a 'settled intention' to stay in your area.

- 'Appreciable period' is not defined. If the DWP suggests appreciable period is a fixed period of time, this should be challenged. Appreciable period is linked with 'settled intention'.
- You have a 'settled intention' in the UK if you intend to live here for some time. You do not need to intend to live here forever. Lots of factors are considered when deciding if you have a settled intention – for example, registering with a GP or moving your money to the UK.
- The stronger the settled intention, the shorter the appreciable period is likely to be.
- If you go abroad for a holiday, you do not stop being habitually resident in the UK. If you are serving abroad in the UK armed forces or you live with a family member who is, you are still treated as habitually resident in the UK.

European rules mean you may be able to get the the 'daily living component' of PIP if you are habitually resident elsewhere in Europe but still have a strong link to the UK. These are complicated rules and require further advice.

If your claim for PIP is refused because the DWP decides you are not habitually resident, you should get benefits advice to help you challenge the decision. See advicelocal.uk for free sources of advice in your area.

**EXAMPLE**

**The residence rules**

Danielle is a British national who has been living and working in the USA for the last five years. When she is diagnosed with cancer, she gives up her job and her apartment and returns to live permanently with her family in London.

Danielle claims PIP, but her claim is refused on the grounds that she has not been in the UK for two of the last three years.

Two months later, Danielle's consultant tells her that the cancer has spread and that she probably only has a few months to live. She makes a new claim for PIP and asks her consultant to confirm her prognosis on Form SR1.

Danielle is awarded PIP as it is accepted that she is habitually resident.

Because Danielle has a terminal illness, the length of time she has been in Great Britain during the past three years does not matter.

You can continue to get PIP during part of a 'temporary absence' from Great Britain, as the rules treat you as if you are still in Great Britain. The definition of 'temporary absence' is that your absence must not be expected to last longer than a year.

Your PIP continues for the first 13 weeks you are abroad, or for the first 26 weeks if you go abroad specifically for the purpose of getting medical treatment.

If you are abroad in another European country, special European rules mean that you might be able to get the daily living component of PIP for longer.

You should get advice about being absent from Great Britain, and always tell the DWP if you are going abroad.

**What CPAG says**

**If you are affected by the residence rules**

This is a very complicated and fast-changing area of the law. We suggest that if you are refused PIP due to these rules, you get advice to help you to work out if you may be able to successfully challenge the decision. You may also need to check what benefits you may qualify for from another European country.

## Further information

The residence and presence tests for PIP are explained in more detail in CPAG's *Welfare Benefits Handbook* and CPAG's *Benefits for Migrants Handbook*.
On gov.uk there is *Advice for Decision Making*, produced by the DWP for its own staff. Chapter P1 sets out the basic entitlement conditions for PIP and Chapter C2 looks at international issues.

# Chapter 3
# Claims, assessments and getting paid

**This chapter covers:**

1. How do you make a claim?
2. When should you claim?
3. How are you assessed?
4. Getting paid

## What you need to know

- Personal independence payment (PIP) is normally claimed by phone, but there are online and paper options available for some claimants.
- You should claim as soon as you think you might qualify to avoid losing money, as PIP cannot be paid for periods before your claim. You can sometimes make an advance claim.
- After you claim, you are sent a questionnaire to complete about how your health or disability affects you. This is called Form PIP2. Most people must also attend a consultation with a 'healthcare professional'. Consultations can be face to face or by a phone call or video call.
- PIP is usually awarded for a fixed period.
- You are likely to be reassessed about one year before your award is due to end.
- If you are refused PIP, you can ask for the decision to be reconsidered and then appeal.

## 1. How do you make a claim?

### How do you start your claim?

It is best to claim PIP by phone on 0800 917 2222 (textphone: 0800 917 7777). The lines are open between 8am and 5pm, Monday to Friday. The calls are free from most landlines and mobiles, but some providers may charge. If you are worried about the cost of the call, ask the DWP to ring you back.

If you find it hard to use a phone, someone else can ring for you and give the required information, provided you are present during the call and can confirm that the other person is acting with your permission.

If you are unable to manage your own affairs and someone else officially acts for you (for example, a power of attorney), then they should be able to make the claim on your behalf. If you require this help, but do not have a person officially appointed to act for you, someone can apply to the DWP to become your appointee.

If you have difficulty speaking and understanding English, the DWP can arrange for an interpreter to speak to you in your own language during the call.

If you use British Sign Language to communicate, you can make a claim by video call. Go to gov.uk/pip/how-to-claim for details.

If you have a 'terminal illness', someone else can also make a claim on your behalf.

If you cannot make your claim by phone, and have no one to support you, you can use a paper claim form (Form PIP1).

Online claims for PIP are now possible, although intially only in some areas. Check whether you are eligible at apply-for-pip.dwp.gov.uk/eligibility/check-if-eligible. Online claims involve completing both a PIP1 and PIP2 form, therefore do not require a phone call. Online claims are different to the digital PIP2 form.

### What are you asked?

During the call, you are asked for information about yourself to establish your identity and that you meet the basic conditions of entitlement for PIP.

Box A

**Information for your claim**

Have the following information ready for your phone claim:

- full name and date of birth
- national insurance number (if you do not have a national insurance number, you will need to apply for one. The PIP phone line should explain how. You are then sent a PIP claim form.)
- full address, including postcode and contact phone numbers
- details of any communication requirements that you have – for example, if you need letters sent to you in Braille or large print, or recorded on to an audio CD
- nationality and any immigration restrictions
- whether you have been granted European Union pre-settled or settled status
- usual country of residence and details of any time spent abroad, if this was for more than four weeks at a time in the last three years
- dates of current or recent stays in a hospital, hospice or care home
- name, address and phone number of your GP or other 'healthcare professional' who supports you (you are asked to give your consent for the DWP to contact them to get further information about your health condition or disability)
- details of whether you have a condition that affects your mental health, learning, development, behaviour or causes memory problems (in case you require more help or consideration during the assessment process)
- bank or building society account details for payment of PIP

If you cannot establish your identity over the phone, your claim should still be taken, but you may need to provide further information and evidence before it is accepted that you are who you say you are.

At this stage, you are not asked to give more details about your health or disability and how it affects you. The call is likely to take about 15 minutes.

If you do not have all the information listed in Box A when you phone, you can ring back to provide it. Some of the information is required for your claim to be completed. You must provide any required missing information within one month (or a longer period allowed by the DWP) for the claim to be valid and start from the date of your original call. Once all the information is complete, you must declare that it is all correct, as far as you know and believe. The claim is then processed by the DWP.

### Who can complete a paper claim form?

If you are unable to make your claim by phone, you can request a paper claim form (Form PIP1) by phoning 0800 917 2222 (textphone 0800 917 7777). Someone can phone on your behalf if you are present and give your consent to the DWP. If you cannot use the phone and have no one to help you, you can request a claim form by writing to: Freepost DWP PIP 1. This is all you need to write on the envelope and it does not need a stamp. However, requesting a form in this way will delay the date of your claim so it is better to phone and ask for a form if you are able to do this.

You can also ask for a home visit by a DWP visiting officer to help you complete the form if you cannot do this yourself and have no one to help you.

The claim form is personalised for your use only and should not be used by anyone else. You can ask for a large print or Braille version if you are visually impaired.

The claim form asks for the same information as a phone claim and should be returned by post in the envelope provided.

You have one month to complete and return the form for your claim to start on the day of your initial call. If you need longer than this, you should explain why and the time can be extended if it is reasonable to do so.

### Are you terminally ill?

You are treated as 'terminally ill' if you have a progressive disease and you can be reasonably expected to die within 12 months. If you are terminally ill, someone else can make a claim for PIP on your behalf, either by phone or by using a claim form. This can be done with or without your knowledge. The DWP tells you that a claim has been made but does not refer to having a terminal illness. If you are claiming on behalf of someone else, you should therefore tell them that a claim for PIP has been made.

Claims from people who are terminally ill are referred to as special rules claims. The claim itself is slightly different, as you are also asked questions about mobility problems caused by your condition. You, or the person claiming for you, should get Form SR1, confirming your prognosis, from your consultant, GP, nurse or social worker and send it to the DWP (unless one has already been sent within the past six months). Do not delay making your claim because you are waiting for the form; you can send it later.

Instead of a questionnaire and consultation, a different assessment process is normally used if you are terminally ill. The DWP sends your claim information and the SR1 form to the company carrying out the assessment. A healthcare professional then advises the DWP about whether you meet the definition of terminal illness and whether it is likely that you have mobility difficulties. This process allows the decision on your claim to be made more quickly.

An award of PIP on the basis of terminal illness is normally made for three years. If, during this time, you are told that your death can no longer be reasonably expected within 12 months, you should report this as a change in your circumstances. This is because you no longer meet the definition of 'terminal illness' and must be reassessed under the usual rules. Similarly, if you already have an award of PIP and become terminally ill, inform the DWP as soon as possible. Your award can be changed from the date you met the definition of 'terminal illness'. If you do not agree with a decision about your entitlement to PIP, you can challenge it in the normal way (explained in Chapter 7). Someone who has claimed PIP on your behalf without your knowledge can also request a mandatory reconsideration and appeal without your knowledge.

EXAMPLE

**Claims on the grounds of terminal illness**

Brian has just been diagnosed with a terminal illness. He is obviously very upset and is struggling to cope. His wife Nina finds out about PIP and claims by telephone on his behalf. She explains that her husband is terminally ill and gives his basic details. She is asked about his mobility needs and she explains that Brian gets breathless after walking just a few metres, and that this is the reason why he first went to the doctor. She sends Form SR1 to the DWP a week later, and explains to Brian that she has claimed some extra money for him. Four weeks later, Brian is awarded the 'daily living component' and the 'mobility component' of PIP for three years. The letter explaining this does not mention the fact that he is terminally ill.

## 2. When should you claim?

To avoid losing out on money, you should make a claim as soon as you think you may qualify for PIP. This is because you can only be paid from the date of your claim. The only exception to this is if you currently get disability living allowance.

The date of your claim depends on how you make the claim.

- If you claim by phone, the date of claim is the date you call.
- If you make an online claim, the date of claim is the date you submit the PIP1 part.

- If you phone to request that Form PIP1 be sent to you, the date of claim is the date you made the phone request.
- If you write to the DWP requesting that a PIP1 be sent to you, the date of claim is the date the DWP receives this request.

These dates are only confirmed once you provide all of the required information. You usually have one month to do this, though the DWP can extend this date if reasonable.

You cannot normally qualify for PIP until you have met the conditions for the 'daily living component' or 'mobility component' for at least three months. However, you can claim PIP in advance if the DWP thinks you are likely to qualify within three months. You are paid from the date you qualify.

**EXAMPLE**

**The three-month requirement**

Deborah has a stroke on 11 March 2024 and is admitted to hospital. She is discharged on 30 May 2024 and claims PIP later that day. She is assessed as meeting the qualifying conditions from 11 March but is only awarded PIP from 11 June 2024, when she has completed the three-month qualifying period.

## 3. How are you assessed?

To qualify for PIP, you must show that your ability to carry out a range of everyday 'activities' is limited because of your health or disability. Chapters 4, 5 and 6 cover this in more detail.

If your claim shows that you satisfy the basic conditions of entitlement to PIP, you are usually sent a questionnaire (Form PIP2) to complete about how your health or disability affects you, together with explanatory information. The questionnaire is personalised for your use only and cannot be used by anyone else.

Form PIP2 is available as a paper or digital form. The digital form can be emailed either as a PDF attachment or a link to complete online. This is available to most new claimants, in contrast to the full online claim process which is only available in specific geographical areas.

You can request the questionnaire in an alternative format, such as large print or Braille, by phoning the PIP helpline on 0800 917 2222.

Box B

**The questionnaire**

The questionnaire asks for details of:

- professionals you see who can provide information about your condition – for example, your GP, or a doctor, nurse, occupational therapist, physiotherapist, social worker, counsellor or support worker (if there is not room for all of the people who help you, add their details in the 'Additional Information' section at the end of the questionnaire)
- your health condition or disability, including how long this has affected you for, and any medication you take and treatment you have
- the difficulty you have carrying out the everyday activities on which you are assessed. These are:
  - preparing food and cooking
  - eating and drinking
  - managing your treatments and medication
  - washing and bathing
  - managing your toilet needs
  - dressing and undressing
  - speaking and hearing
  - reading
  - mixing with other people
  - making decisions about money
  - going out
  - moving around
- details of any special arrangements that you would need for a face-to-face consultation

If you have claimed on the basis of having a 'terminal illness', you do not need to complete a questionnaire and your claim is passed to a 'healthcare professional' for an assessment.

If you explained that you had a mental health, learning, developmental, behavioural or memory problem when you made your claim, the DWP can also send your claim to be assessed without your having to complete a questionnaire. This is discretionary, so if you are sent a questionnaire you should complete it even if you have one of these conditions, otherwise your claim may be refused.

*What the law says*

**The time limit**

- If you are required to complete and submit a questionnaire, you usually must do so within one month. This can be extended at the DWP's discretion. If you fail to return the questionnaire 'without good reason' within your time limit, you will be issued a decision stating you are not entitled to PIP.
- If you had 'good reason' for being late, you can ask the DWP to look at its decision again (see below and Chapter 7 for more details of how to do this). 'Good reason' can include anything which explains why you were unable to send in the questionnaire on time, such as if you were too unwell, the nature of your disability, or you were abroad or dealing with a domestic emergency. It can also include waiting for an appointment from advice services to help you complete the questionnaire.

*Regulations 8 and 10 Social Security (Personal Independence Payment) Regulations 2013*

If you have not submitted your questionnaire after 20 days, you should receive a reminder letter. If you need more time, phone the PIP helpline on 0800 121 4433 (textphone: 0800 121 4493) and explain your situation. You can be given more time if it is reasonable to do so.

If you receive a decision stating you are not entitled to PIP because you failed to return the questionnaire, you can request a 'mandatory reconsideration' and then appeal. See Chapter 7 for more details on how to do this. Explain why you did not return it and send any evidence that you have confirming this, such as a letter from your GP if you were ill, or an appointment letter if you were waiting for advice. You may also wish to make a new claim, in case the decision is not changed, but it is best to get benefits advice before doing so.

### How should you complete the questionnaire?

It is important to complete the questionnaire as fully as possible and give all the relevant information about your difficulties.

- Read Chapters 4, 5 and 6 of this book so you understand the assessment criteria. In particular, remember that it is not your condition itself that qualifies you for PIP, but how this affects your ability to carry out the specified range of activities. Work out which statements (known as 'descriptors') under each activity you think you satisfy. This will help you to decide what information it is relevant to give.
- If you do not have a firm diagnosis, give a general description of how you are affected by your condition and make sure you explain on the questionnaire what steps are being taken to work out what is causing your symptoms.
- You can include details of carers and relatives who know or help you in the additional information section at the end of the questionnaire. You can also send extra supporting evidence.
- For each activity, explain whether you use or require any aids or appliances, and whether you need help from another person. It is also relevant to state help that you would need to complete the activity, but do not currently receive. It is always helpful to use real-life examples.

- Explain if an activity takes you a long time or puts you at risk, or if you cannot complete it as often as you need to, only to a low standard or with pain.
- If your condition fluctuates, it is important to give information about your good and bad days, how your needs vary during the day, and the proportion of days on which you can and cannot manage the relevant activities. If you do not specifically know how manys days are bad days, words such as 'often' or 'sometimes' may help; however, it is best to be as exact as possible. You may find it helpful to keep a diary, recording how your condition affects you on a daily basis. You can use this to help you complete the questionnaire, or you can send a copy of it with the questionnaire.
- Read the guidance in the questionnaire and explanatory information. This includes useful information and examples of the type of help you may need.
- If you are completing a paper form, complete it clearly and legibly in ink. It will be scanned and sent electronically to a healthcare professional and must be readable. Make sure you read and sign the declaration at the end, confirming that, as far as you are aware, the information you have given is correct.
- If possible, keep a copy, so you can read it before you attend your consultation, and refer to its content if you challenge any decision made later.

### Do you need help completing the questionnaire?

If you need help completing your questionnaire, consult a local advice centre, such as a Citizens Advice. You may also be able to get advice online or by phone from a disability organisation specialising in your condition. To find free advice services in your area, go to advicelocal.uk. A friend, relative or carer could help you complete the questionnaire, provided you sign the declaration.

The PIP helpline (0800 121 4433; textphone 0800 121 4493) can help with any general or basic enquiries you have. Someone from the

DWP may be able to phone you back to give you further advice and help.

If you are unable to complete the questionnaire yourself and cannot get help, the DWP can arrange for you to be visited at home.

*What CPAG says*

**Help with the questionnaire**

If you live with a health condition or disability, often your way of managing becomes 'normal' for you if there is no help available. Due to this, you may underestimate the difficulties you have in relation to the PIP activities. CPAG suggests that you try to get help from a local advice centre to complete the questionnaire. If you are unsure of your ability to explain the help that you need fully, you could take someone who knows you well to help you to explain your needs fully to the advice worker. If waiting for an appointment means that it is going to take you more than one month to return the questionnaire, remember to contact the helpline and ask for an extension of time. You can find your local advice centre by going to advicelocal.uk.

### What evidence should you include?

Your claim may be helped if you send evidence that supports it. If you are not sure whether your evidence is helpful, read through the following list and also check how closely your evidence relates to the activities in the PIP assessment (see Chapters 5 and 6).

Only send photocopies (not the originals) of the documents you have. List the documents you are sending in the box on page 2 of the questionnaire, and send them with the questionnaire in the envelope provided. Do not delay sending your questionnaire while you are waiting for further evidence; you can send the evidence separately when you get it. If you are sending documents as separate sheets, or after returning your questionnaire, make sure you mark them with your name and national insurance number.

Box C

**Evidence to send**

- reports about your condition from relevant professionals
- letters from relevant professionals
- test results from scans, diagnostic tests, hearing or sight tests
- diaries about how your condition affects you, written by yourself or someone who knows you well
- letters from your carer or someone who knows you well
- current prescription list
- certificate of visual impairment
- education, health and care plan (EHCP)
- hospital discharge report

Box D

**Evidence not to send**

- general factsheets about your conditions
- general information about your medication
- anything else that does not relate to your condition or how it affects you

## Who assesses you?

The assessment of whether you satisfy the disability conditions for PIP is carried out in two stages.

- First, you are assessed by a healthcare professional. They decide whether you need to take part in a consultation. The consultation can be face-to-face, over the phone or by video call. The healthcare professional then completes a report and sends it to the DWP.

- Next, your case is looked at by a DWP 'case manager'. They decide whether you are entitled to PIP based on all the evidence, including the healthcare professional's report and your questionnaire. They can seek further evidence or clarification from the healthcare professional or other sources if necessary before making the final decision. The DWP decides whether you are entitled to PIP. The healthcare professional only provides advice to the DWP case manager.

Four private companies carry out PIP medical assessments on behalf of the DWP:

- Maximum UK Services Ltd – covering the North of England and Scotland
- Capita Business Services – covering the Midlands, Wales and Northern Ireland
- Serco – covering South West England
- Ingeus UK Ltd – covering South East England, London and East Anglia

These companies' contracts run until 2029. All assessment providers must operate in accordance with their contracts and service-level agreements with the DWP, and must take into account the detailed guidance on assessments issued by the DWP. Trained healthcare professionals carry out the assessments on behalf of the companies. A healthcare professional could be a:

- registered doctor
- level 1 nurse
- paramedic
- physiotherapist
- occupational therapist
- pharmacist

It is not so important what the healthcare professional's job is, but more important that they are competent in how to assess PIP claimants using the disability criteria.

### What happens at the initial assessment?

The DWP sends a copy of your questionnaire and any other evidence to the relevant assessment provider. The healthcare professional then decides whether further evidence is needed and whether or not a consultation is required.

If the healthcare professional thinks extra evidence would be helpful, they can request a report from your GP, hospital doctor or other healthcare professional listed on your claim form or questionnaire. In practice, this rarely happens; therefore, it is important to request and submit all evidence you think is relevant yourself.

If you have obtained extra evidence that may be helpful to your claim since completing the questionnaire, send a copy to the DWP with a letter asking for it to be forwarded to the assessment provider for consideration. Send this to the address where you sent your PIP claim form.

## Who does not need to attend a consultation?

Most people must attend a consultation. However, in some circumstances, the assessor can complete an assessment and send a report to the DWP based on the evidence in the papers, without seeing you. This should always happen if your claim is on the basis of a 'terminal illness' and you have confirmed this with appropriate evidence. If you are terminally ill, your assessment should be completed and returned to the DWP more quickly than other claims.

You may not need to attend a face-to-face consultation if you provide medical evidence that you would find the consultation distressing.

## Attending a consultation

All assessment providers use healthcare professionals based at dedicated assessment centres, or in local NHS or private health centres or clinics. If you are asked to attend a face-to-face consultation, you are usually required to attend at the place where the healthcare professional is based. This should be accessible for disabled people, and by public transport within a maximum of 90 minutes' travelling time. If you are unable, or would find it difficult, to travel because of your condition, you can request a phone, video or home consultation. Explain why you need this and support your request with medical or other evidence. If an alternative to a face-to-face consultation is refused, you can complain to the assessment provider; however, you should still make every effort to attend the consultation, otherwise your claim may be refused.

You should receive a letter with details of your appointment and what to take with you if it is a face-to-face consultation, including proof of identity and any new evidence you may have about your health condition or disability. You must be given at least seven days' written notice of your appointment (unless you agree to accept shorter notice).

If you cannot attend, phone the number on your appointment letter and ask for another appointment. You can also phone if you have any special requirements, including if you need an interpreter or if you want a consultation with a person of a specific gender.

The cost of your travel expenses can be reimbursed. If you take someone with you, their travel expenses can also be reimbursed. You should be sent a claim form with your appointment letter, but you cannot claim in advance. You are paid by cheque or directly into your bank account. You can claim for the cost of public transport or travel by car (including any parking charges). If you need to travel by taxi because you cannot use public transport or it is not available, phone the number on your appointment letter in advance about this.

### What happens at the consultation?

The consultation is with a trained healthcare professional. You can ask for someone else, such as a friend, relative, carer or support worker, to take part in the consultation. As well as giving you support, they can join you in the discussion and help explain how your condition or disability affects you. If you want to take more than one person with you, you should ask about this in advance by phoning the number on your appointment letter.

The aim of the consultation is to enable the healthcare professional to gather evidence about how your health or disability affects you, so they can advise the DWP which descriptors apply to you.

They should speak to you politely and clearly, asking you open questions and giving you the time and opportunity to explain properly how your health condition or disability affects you.

Although they will probably need to record information on a computer system during the consultation, this should not be done at the expense of listening to you or maintaining regular eye contact while you are speaking.

The assessment provider can make an audio recording of your phone or face-to-face consultation. You must request this in advance. Alternatively, you can make your own audio recording. You do not need to request this in advance, nor do you need permission. You are not able to make a video recording.

There is no set length of time for the consultation, but it may typically take about an hour.

### *What questions are you asked?*

- You are asked about your condition, including what it is, when it began, what symptoms you experience and whether they fluctuate, and what treatment you have had or are having, including any medication you take.
- You are also asked about your work history and social life, such as where you live, whether your home has adaptations, whether anyone lives with you and supports you, and the leisure and social activities you do or can no longer do.
- You are then asked questions about how your illness or disability affects your everyday life. This is usually done by asking you to talk through a typical day: explaining what you do and what difficulties you have carrying out everyday tasks, including washing and dressing, preparing food and eating, communicating with others and getting out and about, which may include shopping and any hobbies.

### *Will you be examined?*

If appropriate, the healthcare professional may carry out a short medical examination relevant to your condition. You must give your consent to this and may be asked to recline on an examination couch. You should never be required to remove your underwear or to undergo a breast, rectal or genital examination.

Box E

**Preparing for the consultation**

- Read your questionnaire and any other evidence you have submitted before you attend. This will help ensure that the information you give during the consultation is consistent.
- Read Chapters 4, 5 and 6 of this book, so you are familiar with the descriptors you satisfy. When you answer questions about a typical day and how your condition affects you, focus on showing that you satisfy the descriptors.
- Provide information about any aids and appliances you use and the help you need from other people. If your condition fluctuates, give information about your good and bad days, and the proportion of days on which you can and cannot undertake relevant activities. Make sure you explain difficulties with managing the activities at certain times of the day.
- Focus on the difficulties you face. Even if you manage to carry out certain tasks, explain if, and how, these are difficult for you. Consider whether you can complete a task safely, to an acceptable standard, repeatedly and within a reasonable time period. Refer to Chapter 4 for more information about these terms. Remember that the test is not whether you get help, but whether you need help.
- Prepare what you want to say about your condition, your symptoms, your typical day, and the difficulties you face with everyday tasks. Bear in mind that the healthcare professional is unlikely to be a specialist in your condition, so you may need to explain its nature and the symptoms. Take details of your medication and any new evidence that is relevant to your claim.
- Take someone with you if you want support. They may also be able to give useful information about your difficulties. Talk through the above points with them beforehand, so you are both clear about what you want to say.

### *What observations are made?*

Throughout the consultation, the healthcare professional makes their own observations about your physical and psychological abilities and limitations, including on how you stand, sit, move around, answer questions and behave.

Box F

**Travelling to the consultation**

- If you are required to take part in a face-to-face consultation, allow plenty of time for the journey, so you arrive in time and are as relaxed as possible.
- Explain if you have had to take extra medication to manage to get to the consultation. The healthcare professional assessing you is likely to ask you how you travelled to the assessment centre as part of their observations – for example, how far you had to walk, whether you travelled by public transport and whether you travelled alone.

### *Are you unhappy with the consultation?*

If you are unhappy with the way you were treated during the consultation, you can make a complaint. You may be unhappy about how you were spoken to, listened to or examined, or about the venue or waiting times. You should be given information about the complaints procedure at the end of your consultation.

You should normally receive a full response within 20 working days.

Making a complaint should not affect your claim for PIP.

### What happens if you do not attend the consultation?

If you do not attend or participate in a consultation and do not have a good reason, your claim may be refused. If you cannot attend an appointment, you should phone the assessment provider on the number provided as soon as possible to explain why.

If you receive a decision stating you are not entitled to PIP because you failed to attend or participate in a consultation, you can ask for a mandatory reconsideration and then appeal. See Chapter 7 for more details on how to do this. You should explain why you did not attend or participate and send evidence confirming this, such as a letter from your GP if you were ill. You should also get advice about making a new claim, in case the decision is not changed.

*What the law says*

**Failing to attend the consultation**

- You must have received at least seven days' written notice of your appointment (unless you agreed to shorter notice).
- 'Good reason' can include anything which explains why you were unable to attend the consultation, such as if you were too ill or disabled, you were abroad or you were dealing with a domestic emergency.

*Regulations 9 and 10 Social Security (Personal Independence Payment) Regulations 2013*

### The healthcare professional's report

After the consultation, the healthcare professional writes a report for the DWP, setting out their findings and advice on which descriptors you satisfy.

The report also advises on the probable timescale over which your condition is likely to affect you. This information is used by the DWP to decide whether your ability to carry out everyday activities will be affected for at least a year, the duration of your award and when you should be reassessed.

You can request a copy of the report from the DWP, which may help if you wish to challenge the decision made on your PIP claim.

If there are significant mistakes made in the report, you can also make a complaint.

### When are you reassessed?

You can be reassessed for PIP at any time; however, this is likely to happen when you have an award of PIP and:

- you report a change in your condition or needs
- it is almost the date when your current award ends (usually 12 months before)

You must complete a new questionnaire (though it may be a shorter form) and are likely to be asked to attend another consultation.

If you have been refused PIP in the past, you can make a new claim at any time, and are assessed in the usual way. You should consider doing this if your condition has deteriorated and your needs have increased.

## 4. Getting paid

### The decision on your claim

The DWP writes to you, informing you of its decision on your claim for PIP. This includes the decision maker's reasoning and details of which descriptors you satisfy. The decision letter also explains how you are paid and your duty to report relevant changes in your circumstances, such as if your condition changes, or if you go into hospital or a care home.

If your claim has been refused or you think you should have been awarded a higher amount, you can ask for a 'mandatory reconsideration' and then appeal. There are details of how to do this in the decision letter and more information about this in Chapter 7.

### How much personal independence payment do you get?

**Amount of PIP (2024/25 rates)**

| Component | Standard weekly rate | Enhanced weekly rate |
|---|---|---|
| Daily living component | £72.65 | £108.55 |
| Mobility component | £28.70 | £75.75 |

### How are you paid?

PIP can be paid into a bank account, building society or credit union account. It is usually paid every four weeks in arrears on the same day of the week that your decision was made, although this can be changed by the DWP. Awards of PIP on the basis of terminal illness are paid weekly in advance. If someone is acting on your behalf (an 'appointee'), your PIP is paid directly to them.

PIP can also be paid to a third party, if the DWP considers that is necessary to protect your interests.

If you receive the enhanced rate of the 'mobility component', it can be paid directly to the Motability scheme to lease a car or other vehicle, rather than being paid directly to you.

### How long is personal independence payment awarded for?

- You are given a short-term fixed award of up to two years if your condition is likely to improve within that period.
- You are given a longer-term fixed award if your condition is less likely to change or might be expected to worsen.
- Awards on the basis of 'terminal illness' are normally made for three years.
- An indefinite award can be made if a fixed-term award would be inappropriate. These awards are still reviewed, usually every 10 years. The DWP uses a short review questionnaire (Form AR2) for people with indefinite awards.

### What happens at the end of your award?

If your PIP award is made for two years or more, you are usually contacted one year before your award is due to end. You are asked to complete a questionnaire about the daily living and mobility 'activities' and may need to attend another consultation. The process is similar to the new claim process explained earlier in this chapter, though you may be sent a shorter questionnaire asking whether your condition has changed (Form AR1).

If you do not return the questionnaire, or attend or participate in the consultation and you are not accepted as having a good reason, your award of PIP ends. You can challenge this decision, but should also get advice about making a new claim in case your challenge is not successful.

If you have an award shorter than two years, you may not be sent another questionnaire to complete. In these cases, the DWP should contact you around three months before your award ends, to invite you to make a new claim. You do not need to wait to be contacted, and you may wish to consider making a new claim earlier, to ensure the review process is completed before your current award ends.

If no decision is made on renewal or review claims before your current award ends, your PIP may stop. The DWP is currently automatically extending PIP awards by a year where a review is due but has not been completed; however, this is a temporary policy and could end at any time.

## Further information

CPAG's *Welfare Benefits Handbook* contains detailed information about the PIP claims process, with references to the legislation and the most important caselaw.
On gov.uk there is information about how to claim PIP, and also a *PIP Handbook* giving more details of how to claim and what happens. The *PIP Assessment Guide* contains details of how assessors must carry out consultations.

# Chapter 4
# Meeting the assessment criteria

**This chapter covers:**

1. The assessment criteria and qualifying period
2. Activities, descriptors and points
3. How are the descriptors applied?

**What you need to know**

- Personal independence payment (PIP) has two 'components': a 'daily living component' and a 'mobility component'. You can qualify for one or both components, which are each paid at a standard or enhanced rate.
- To qualify for either component, you must normally satisfy the assessment criteria for at least a year.
- You are assessed on your ability to carry out 10 daily living 'activities' and two mobility 'activities'.
- Special rules apply if you have a 'terminal illness'. You can qualify for PIP immediately and automatically satisfy the assessment crieria for the enhanced rate of the daily living component.

## 1. The assessment criteria and qualifying period

PIP has two 'components': a 'daily living component' and a 'mobility component'. You may qualify for one or both components.

Each component can be paid at either a standard or enhanced (higher) rate, depending on how your condition affects you. It is not your condition or disability itself that qualifies you for PIP, but how it affects your ability to carry out specified activities.

You are assessed on your ability to carry out 10 daily living 'activities' and two mobility 'activities'.

This chapter lists the activities and explains the assessment criteria.

Chapter 5 explains the daily living activities in more detail and Chapter 6 explains the mobility activities.

## The qualifying period

To qualify for PIP, you must have met the assessment criteria for a particular component or rate for three months before the date of your claim. You must also be likely to meet the criteria for a further nine months after the date of your claim. This pair of requirements is known as 'the required period condition'.

You can claim PIP during the three-month qualifying period, but your entitlement cannot start until the three months have elapsed. The nine-month forward condition immediately follows on from the day you first qualify.

**EXAMPLES**

**The qualifying period**

Alexander has had a visual impairment since he was born. It greatly restricts his everyday activities. When he claims PIP, he satisfies both the three-month and the nine-month qualifying period.

Jane breaks her leg. Three months later, she claims PIP. The DWP decides that, although she has satisfied the criteria for an award for three months, she is unlikely to satisfy them for a further nine months because her leg will have healed before then. She is refused PIP.

For each day you get PIP, you must still be likely to satisfy the criteria for a further nine months. If you ask for your award to be looked at again as you think you qualify for a different component or a higher rate, you must show that you have satisfied the conditions for at least three months and are likely to satisfy them for a further nine months.

EXAMPLE

**The qualifying period: condtion deteriorates**

Samir gets the standard rate of the daily living component. His condition deteriorates and he immediately asks for his award to be looked at again.

The DWP accepts that his higher level of needs is likely to last for a qualifying period and decides that he will qualify for the enhanced rate of both components, and his award increases from three months after his condition got worse.

### When does the qualifying period not apply?

You may be awarded PIP without having to satisfy the qualifying period in the following situations.

- You claim PIP on the basis of having a 'terminal illness'. You do not have to meet the three-month qualifying period or the nine-month forward condition.
- You claim PIP within two years of any previous entitlement ending (or within one year if you are pension age or older). You do not have to satisfy the three-month qualifying condition to requalify for the same component you were getting before, provided you have the same condition or a new condition that has developed as a result of it. You must still show that you are likely to meet the criteria for nine months from the date of your new claim.

- You are transferring from disability living allowance to PIP. You do not need to meet the three-month qualifying condition. You must still show that you are likely to meet the nine-month forward condition.

**EXAMPLES**

**Getting personal independence payment without satisfying the qualifying period**

Tom has been diagnosed with pancreatic cancer. He submits Form SR1 from his GP, confirming death can be expected within 12 months.

Tom is automatically entitled to the daily living component enhanced rate from the date he makes the claim, without having to satisfy the three-month qualifying condition.

Judith was getting both components of PIP, but this stopped 18 months ago when her condition went into remission. It has flared up again and she reclaims.

The DWP decides that Judith is entitled to both components again straight away, without having to satisfy the three-month qualifying period. If Judith had been receiving just one component, she could only qualify for the other component after satisfying the criteria for three months.

Declan has arthritis and currently gets disability living allowance. He is invited to make a claim for PIP.

As Declan has been getting disability living allowance, he does not need to meet the three-month qualifying period, but must still provide evidence that he is likely to meet the nine-month forward condition.

## 2. Activities, descriptors and points

Your entitlement to PIP is assessed on your ability to carry out 10 daily living 'activities' and two mobility 'activities'.

### What are the activities?

*What the law says*

**Daily living activities**

- preparing food
- taking nutrition
- managing therapy or monitoring a health condition
- washing and bathing
- managing toilet needs or incontinence
- dressing and undressing
- communicating verbally
- reading and understanding signs, symbols and words
- engaging with other people face to face
- making budgeting decisions

**Mobility activities**

- planning and following journeys
- moving around

*Schedule 1 Social Security (Personal Independence Payment) Regulations 2013*

### What are the descriptors?

Each activity is described by a number of statements (called 'descriptors') that reflect different levels of ability to carry out the activity. Each descriptor is given a number of points. The greater the level of difficulty described, the higher the number of points.

For example, the activity 'managing toilet needs or incontinence' has six descriptors.

**Managing toilet needs or incontinence**

| Descriptor | Points |
|---|---|
| Can manage toilet needs or incontinence unaided. | 0 |
| Needs to use an aid or appliance to be able to manage toilet needs or incontinence. | 2 |
| Needs supervision or prompting to be able to manage toilet needs. | 2 |
| Needs assistance to be able to manage toilet needs. | 4 |
| Needs assistance to be able to manage incontinence of either bladder or bowel. | 6 |
| Needs assistance to be able to manage incontinence of both bladder and bowel. | 8 |

You only score points for one descriptor under each activity. You can, however, score points for any or all of the activities.

The points you score for the daily living activities and the mobility activities are added up separately.

### How many points do you need?

You must score at least eight points to qualify for either component.

- If you score eight, nine, 10 or 11 points in total for the daily living activities, you are entitled to the standard rate of the 'daily living component'. If you score 12 points or more, you are entitled to the enhanced rate.
- If you score eight, nine, 10 or 11 points in total for the mobility activities, you are entitled to the standard rate of the 'mobility component'. If you score 12 points or more, you are entitled to the enhanced rate.

EXAMPLE

**Scoring points**

Pat has a physical disability and uses a wheelchair outdoors. Her condition also makes a number of daily living activities more difficult for her. She scores the following points for the daily living activities:

- two points for preparing food (descriptor 1(b), 'needs to use an aid or appliance to be able to either prepare or cook a simple meal')
- three points for washing and bathing (descriptor 4(e), 'needs assistance to be able to get in or out of a bath or shower')
- two points for managing toilet needs (descriptor 5(b), 'needs to use an aid or appliance to be able to manage toilet needs or incontinence')
- two points for dressing and undressing (descriptor 6(d), 'needs assistance to be able to dress or undress their lower body')
- no points for the other daily living activities, which she can manage without help

This gives her a total of nine points, which entitles her to the standard rate of the daily living component.

In addition, she scores 12 points for the mobility activity, moving around (descriptor 2(e), 'can stand and then move more than one metre but no more than 20 metres, either aided or unaided'). This entitles her to the enhanced rate of the mobility component.

### Do you have a terminal illness?

For PIP, you are treated as having a 'terminal illness' if you are not expected to live longer than 12 months.

Special rules apply in these situations.

If you are terminally ill, you automatically qualify for the daily living component of PIP at the enhanced rate. It does not matter whether you currently have any problems with daily living activities or for how long you have been unwell. You do not have to wait three months to qualify.

You must still score at least eight points for the two mobility activities to get the mobility component of PIP if you are terminally ill, but it does not matter how long your mobility needs have lasted or are expected to last. You need not have met the assessment criteria for three months before you qualify for the mobility component. The information given when your claim was made and any other evidence is used to decide if you satisfy the criteria.

EXAMPLE

**Terminal illness**

Madelena had breast cancer which was thought to be in remission. However, she has just been told that the cancer has spread and caused a brain tumour, and that she has less than a year to live.

Other than severe headaches some mornings, she currently has no symptoms that affect her ability to undertake the daily living activities in the PIP assessment. Madelena claims PIP, and is awarded the daily living component at the enhanced rate from the date of her claim.

## 3. How are the descriptors applied?

Chapter 5 has more details on the daily living 'activities' and Chapter 6 has more details on the mobility 'activities'. Both chapters list and examine the 'descriptors' and points under each activity.

This section covers the general rules and issues about how the descriptors are applied.

## Does your condition fluctuate?

If your condition or needs fluctuate, you can still meet the criteria for an award of PIP. Although you must satisfy the criteria over the required period of 12 months (as discussed in the first section of this chapter), you do not have to do this on every day, just for the majority of the days.

*What the law says*

### Fluctuating conditions

- If one descriptor in an activity is satisfied on more than 50 per cent of the days in the 'required period', that descriptor applies.
- If two or more descriptors in the same activity are satisfied on more than 50 per cent of the days, the one that scores the highest points applies.
- If none of the descriptors in an activity are satisfied on more than 50 per cent of the days but, combined, two or more scoring descriptors are satisfied on more than 50 per cent of the days, the scoring descriptor that is satisfied on the highest proportion of days applies. If two descriptors apply on the same number of days, the highest scoring one applies.

*Regulation 7 Social Security (Personal Independence Payment) Regulations 2013*

It is often difficult to accurately assess the number of days on which you satisfy a particular descriptor. Keeping a diary may help you identify a pattern over a period of time, and this can also be submitted as part of your PIP claim.

You must be *likely* to satisfy a descriptor on any particular day. If your future condition is uncertain because, for example, you might have further treatment and the outcome of it is unknown, or because the nature or speed of your recovery is in doubt, the assessment should be based on the continuing effect of your current condition. It should disregard the effect of further treatment or recovery.

The descriptors should apply on a particular day if they apply at any time during the day, unless you only have difficulty for a very small part of the day. There is no distinction between the needs you have during the day and the needs you have at night.

**EXAMPLES**

**Fluctuating conditions**

Tracey suffers with chronic fatigue. She is unable to walk more than 50 metres unaided as she often needs to stop due to her fatigue, on more than 50 per cent of days. On the other days, when she feels stronger and less tired, she can walk over 200 metres. This situation is likely to persist for over a year.

In these circumstances, descriptor 2(c) of the moving around activity applies ('can stand and then move unaided more than 20 metres but no more than 50 metres'). This scores eight points and entitles Tracey to the standard rate of the 'mobility component'.

Shae has arthritis, which particularly affects her hands. She has had the condition for two years and it is unlikely to get better. On approximately 40 per cent of days, her arthritis prevents her from preparing a simple meal without assistance: she is unable to chop up vegetables, open packaging and carry things in the kitchen due to stiffness and pain. On approximately 15 per cent of days, her arthritis flares up so badly that she is unable to prepare any food or cook at all, and relies on someone else to make all of her meals.

Although she does not satisfy any of the individual preparing food descriptors for 50 per cent of days, she satisfies either descriptors 1(e) ('needs assistance to either prepare or cook a simple meal') or 1(f) ('cannot prepare and cook food') on more than 50 per cent of days in total. In these circumstances, descriptor 1(e) is awarded because it applies for the highest proportion of the days.

## What do the terms mean?

Many of the words and phrases used in the PIP descriptors are defined in the regulations, which means that ordinary words like 'cook', 'stand', 'assistance' and 'supervision' are given specific meanings. A full list is in Appendix 2. When deciding which descriptors apply to you, first check whether there are any special definitions of the words used in the descriptor.

EXAMPLE

**Meaning of terms**

Henri walks with prosthetic legs. He is also an athlete who regularly runs at athletic meetings using blades.

Henri scores 12 points for mobility descriptor 2(f) ('cannot either aided or unaided stand or move more than one metre'), which entitles him to the enhanced rate of the mobility component. Although he can move around without difficulty, he is unable to 'stand' in accordance with the definition of that word, which is 'to stand upright with at least one biological foot on the ground'. If he only had one leg, however, he would be able to 'stand'.

## Do you use an aid or appliance?

*What the law says*

**Aids and appliances**

An 'aid or appliance' is any device, including a prosthesis, that improves, provides or replaces an impaired physical or mental function.

*Regulation 2 Social Security (Personal Independence Payment) Regulations 2013*

Box A

**Examples of aids and appliances**

- artificial limb (prosthesis)
- walking stick
- specialist cutlery
- spiked chopping board
- dosette box
- alarms
- grab rails
- raised toilet seat
- incontinence pads
- stoma
- shoe aids
- front-fastening bra
- shower seat
- magnifying glass
- hearing aid

You score points for most of the daily living activities if you need an aid or appliance to complete the activity. It is therefore important to identify within your questionnaire which aids or appliances you use, or would need to use, to complete the activity. Aids and appliances can include some items used by people without disabilities, like an electric can opener and jar opener. They must be something you use before or during an activity, to enable you to complete it.

An aid or appliance you do not use is still taken into account if you could be reasonably expected to use it to complete the activity. Some factors that may be relevant include:

- if you have been advised to use it by a medical professional
- if it is available to you (taking into account cost and whether it can actually be provided)
- if it is practical for you to use – for example, it can be stored at your home

Note that you can score points for the planning and following journeys activity if you need an assistance dog (a dog trained to guide or assist someone with a sensory impairment) or an orientation aid (a specialist aid designed to help disabled people follow a route safely) but cannot score points for needing any other aid or appliance.

EXAMPLE

**Aids and appliances**

Martha had a stroke six months ago that has left her with weakness and restricted movement down the right side of her body.

She needs to use a spiked chopping board to prepare and cook a meal. She also needs to use a long-handled sponge to wash her right side. She has a frame around the toilet to enable her to get on and off the toilet, and needs to wear clothes without buttons and shoes without laces, and uses a grabber and a long shoe horn to enable her to dress and undress.

Martha should score two points for each of the descriptors:

- 1(b) ('needs to use an aid or appliance to be able to cook a simple meal')
- 4(b) ('needs to use an aid or appliance to be able to wash or bathe')
- 5(b) ('needs to use an aid or appliance to manage toilet needs')
- 6(b) ('needs to use an aid or appliance to dress or undress').

This entitles her to the standard rate of the 'daily living component'.

### Do you need help from other people?

The help you need from another person to complete an activity is taken into account. The descriptors mainly refer to three types of help: assistance, supervision and prompting. For most daily living activities there is also a descriptor describing your needs if you cannot manage the activity at all, even with these kinds of help.

*What the law says*

## Help from other people

- **'Assistance'** is 'physical intervention by another person and does not include speech'. You must require the physical presence and intervention of another person for at least some of the activity. For example, someone physically helping you get in or out of the bath or shower. It does not include someone doing the whole activity for you.
- **'Supervision'** is 'the continuous presence of another person for the purpose of ensuring the claimant's safety'. You must need someone with you throughout the time you are carrying out the activity to make sure you stay safe. You need supervision if there is a 'real risk' of harm while carrying out the activity, considering both the likelihood and seriousness of the harm. You may score points even if you would not come to harm most days if left unsupervised. For example, if you have a condition that means you are at risk of choking whilst eating, even if you will not choke every day. This interpretation was not previously accepted. The DWP is looking again at decisions made since 9 March 2017 to check they are correct and change any awards it discovers are wrong. Get advice if you think you should have scored more points.
- **'Prompting'** is 'reminding, encouraging or explaining by another person'. In other words, you must need someone to do one or more of these things to help you complete the activity. For example, someone verbally encouraging you to change your clothes if you have low motivation to do so. Prompting does not necessarily involve the physical presence of another person, so someone could prompt you through a phone call.

*Part 1, Schedule 1 Social Security (Personal Independence Payment) Regulations 2013*

You are assessed on whether you need help, not whether you actually receive it or whether it is available to you. So, if you have to undertake an activity yourself because you have no one to help you, but you find it a struggle and really need someone to help you, you should state the kind of help that you need and score points for the relevant descriptors.

For some people, it may be difficult to recognise the help you need if you are used to managing on your own. However, for the purpose of your PIP claim, you should do your best to identify and explain the help and support you need.

EXAMPLE

**Help from other people**

Bettina has multiple sclerosis. She lives on her own and has no one to help her.

Bettina cooks for herself, but finds it difficult to prepare and cut up food, and lift pots and pans. She mainly eats ready meals, which she heats in her microwave. She also makes sure her meals consist of small pieces, so she does not have to cut her food when eating.

She uses the shower every day, but it takes her a very long time because of her poor co-ordination. The same applies to her dressing and undressing.

Bettina scores four points for descriptor 1(e) ('needs assistance to either prepare or cook a simple meal'); two points for descriptor 2(b)(iii) ('needs assistance to be able to cut up food'); four points for descriptor 4(f) ('needs assistance to be able to wash their body between the shoulders and waist'); and four points for descriptor 6(e) ('needs assistance to be able to dress or undress their upper body'). This gives her a total of 14 points, which qualifies her for the enhanced rate of the daily living component.

**EXAMPLE**

**Help from other people**

Tony has severe memory problems and depression. He regularly needs to be reminded and encouraged to cook a meal, to eat, to take his medication, to bathe and dress himself, and to pay his bills. Relatives and friends pop in to see him or ring him nearly every day about all of these things.

He scores two points for descriptor 1(d) ('needs prompting to be able to prepare or cook a simple meal'); four points for descriptor 2(d) ('needs prompting to be able to take nutrition'); one point for descriptor 3(b)(ii) ('needs prompting to be able to manage medication'); two points for descriptor 4(c) ('needs prompting to be able to wash or bathe'); two points for descriptor 6(c)(i) ('needs prompting to be able to dress or undress'); and two points for descriptor 10(b) ('needs prompting to be able to make complex budgeting decisions'). This gives a total of 13 points, so he is entitled to the enhanced rate of the daily living component.

## Can you undertake an activity reliably?

*What the law says*

**Reliability**

You must only be assessed as able to carry out an activity at the level described by a descriptor if you can do so:

- safely – in a manner unlikely to cause harm to you or another person, either during the activity or after it is completed
- to an acceptable standard – applying a test of what would normally be considered to be reasonable
- repeatedly – as often as is reasonably required for that particular activity
- in a reasonable time period – in no more than twice the time it would normally take a person without a disability or health condition to carry out the activity

*Regulation 4(2A) and (4) Social Security (Personal Independence Payment) Regulations 2013*

In order for a descriptor to apply, you must be able to undertake the relevant activity reliably. This means you must complete it safely, to an acceptable standard, repeatedly and in a reasonable time period. If you cannot do that, you are treated for PIP as unable to complete the activity.

When considering whether you can manage something safely, both the likelihood of any harm occurring and the severity of the consequences if it did occur should be taken into account. You should not be expected to restrict the way in which you carry out an activity (for example, how long you shower for) in order to do it safely.

In considering whether you can manage an activity to an acceptable standard, the benchmark is whether the standard you manage is 'good enough'. For example, if you can only put on very loose clothes without zips or buttons and must wear slippers as you cannot manage shoes and socks without help from someone else, this would not be dressing to an acceptable standard.

If you cannot complete an activity as often as it should be completed, then you cannot meet the repeatedly criteria and should score points for whichever descriptor describes the type of help you require. The definition of repeatedly means that if you need help with an activity for part of a day, that day should count as one in which you score points for the fluctuating conditions rules explained above. The exception to this is if you only need help for a very small amount of time. For example, if your condition causes one brief dizzy spell on some days, meaning you need to sit down for a few moments to recover, that would be unlikely to allow you to score any points unless there are other effects on your ability to carry out the activities. How often you need to complete an activity is not specified; instead, you need to consider how often it would normally be completed. For example, someone would usually prepare food three times a day, but only cook once a day.

Because of the way that repeatedly is defined, you may count as unable to perform an activity if you are unable to stop it – for example, if you compulsively eat or wash.

If you have to take frequent rests or follow a set routine, you may need an aid or help from someone else to manage activities within a reasonable time period. You should think carefully about what kind of help would allow you to manage the activity in less than twice the time someone without your condition would take. Some activities have reasonable time periods listed in guidance – for example, the DWP considers 30 metres per minute a reasonable time period for the moving around activity.

**EXAMPLES**

**Reliability**

Ruth can walk 20–50 metres once or twice a day using a walking stick. Afterwards, she gets too tired and is in too much pain to be able to walk more than 20 metres again on the same day.

She does not satisfy mobility descriptor 2(d) ('can walk more than 20 metres but no more than 50 metres') because she cannot do so repeatedly. It would be reasonable to expect someone to be able to walk such a distance more than twice in a day. Instead, she satisfies descriptor 2(e) ('can walk more than one metre but no more than 20 metres') because she can manage this several times a day. This scores 12 points and she is entitled to the enhanced rate of the mobility component.

---

Sarwan has obsessive compulsive disorder. His ritualised behaviour means it takes him several hours to complete short journeys because he only feels safe if he follows certain routes using certain buses at particular times. Help from another person would not change this, as he refuses to change his routine even if a family member is with him.

He satisfies mobility descriptor 1(e) ('cannot undertake any journey because it would cause him overwhelming psychological distress') because he is unable to complete a journey in a reasonable time without overwhelming distress. He qualifies for the mobility component at the standard rate.

**EXAMPLE**

**Reliability**

Frank has severe depression. He only eats soup or crisps if no one is around to encourage him to eat a proper meal. Descriptor 2(d) ('needs prompting to be able to take nutrition') applies because his diet without being prompted would not be taking nutrition to an acceptable standard.

*What CPAG says*

**Applying the descriptors**

PIP's system of assessing entitlement means that you score points for a descriptor if you cannot 'reliably' manage an activity without help – even if only one of the four factors is missing. You should be very clear about how you would be unsafe, how long the activity would take, whether you could manage as often as you need to and to what standard you could manage an activity without help. This should help you to make sure that the points you are given in the assessment reflect the kind of help that you need, whether you can currently get that help or not.

## Further information

CPAG's *Welfare Benefits Handbook* contains detailed information about the PIP assessment, with references to the legislation and the most important caselaw.
The *PIP Assessment Guide* (on gov.uk) for assessment providers explains how to decide which descriptors are satisfied. Part 2 of this guide considers the reliability criteria.
Disability Rights UK has produced a useful booklet about claiming PIP, with information about the assessment criteria. You can download it at disabilityrightsuk.org/personal-independence-payment-pip.

# Chapter 5
# The daily living activities

This chapter covers:

1. Do you have difficulty preparing and cooking food?
2. Do you have difficulty eating and drinking?
3. Do you have difficulty taking medication, undergoing treatment at home, or keeping an eye on your health?
4. Do you have difficulty washing and bathing?
5. Do you have difficulty using the toilet?
6. Do you have difficulty getting dressed or undressed?
7. Do you have difficulty speaking and hearing?
8. Do you have difficulty reading?
9. Do you have difficulty mixing with other people?
10. Do you have difficulty managing money?

## What you need to know

- There are 10 daily living 'activities' in the personal independence payment (PIP) assessment.
- Each activity contains a series of statements (called 'descriptors') which score a certain number of points.
- If you score at least eight points, you are awarded the 'daily living component' paid at the standard rate. If you score 12 points or more or you are 'terminally ill', you are awarded the enhanced rate.
- Only the activities explained in this chapter are taken into account. Any other help you need is not taken into account.

*What CPAG says*

**The daily living activities**

The choice of only 10 daily living activities may make it easy for you to work out whether you are entitled to PIP or not. The test is what help you reasonably need, not what help you have available or actually receive. This makes it important for you to think about the coping strategies you need to manage these activities.

## 1. Do you have difficulty preparing and cooking food?

*What the law says*

**Activity one: preparing food**

| Descriptor | Points |
|---|---|
| (a) Can prepare and cook a simple meal unaided. | 0 |
| (b) Needs to use an aid or appliance to be able to either prepare or cook a simple meal. | 2 |
| (c) Cannot cook a simple meal using a conventional cooker but is able to do so using a microwave. | 2 |
| (d) Needs prompting to be able to either prepare or cook a simple meal. | 2 |
| (e) Needs supervision or assistance to either prepare or cook a simple meal. | 4 |
| (f) Cannot prepare and cook food. | 8 |

*Schedule 1, Part 2 Social Security (Personal Independence Payment) Regulations 2013*

### What is looked at?

This 'activity' looks at your ability to prepare and cook a 'simple meal'.

Box A

**A simple meal**

A 'simple meal' is a meal for one person, made using fresh ingredients. This means that if you can only make ready meals, and cannot open tins or peel and chop vegetables, you should score some points for this activity. Dietary needs, religious beliefs or cultural preferences are not taken into account.

'Prepare' means to make food ready for cooking or eating. You must be able to peel and chop vegetables as part of this. If you must use pre-prepared vegetables due to your condition, you arguably score points for needing assistance.

You only need to be able to prepare and cook sufficient food for one person. If you have a large family and cannot lift large pans of food, or get tired chopping enough vegetables for everyone, this is not taken into account. If you have a low oven and you find it difficult to bend down to use it, this is also not taken into account. Only cooking tasks at waist height or above are assessed.

There are many different aids that you might use to help you prepare food or cook a meal. For example, if you have problems with your hands, you may need to use an adapted vegetable peeler. Single lever arm taps or lightweight pots and pans are less likely to be accepted as aids. A perching stool is unlikely to count as an aid unless your condition means you are only able to stand for very short periods. Remember, only things you need to use because of your health condition or disability count as aids to help you score points.

EXAMPLE

**Perching stool as an aid**

Fliss has peripheral neuropathy, which causes numbness and muscle weakness in her legs. She cannot stand for long without help. Social services have provided her with a perching stool so she can sit while preparing food. The DWP concludes it is reasonable Fliss would have difficulties standing for long and agrees the perching stool is an aid.

EXAMPLES

**Kitchen aids**

Bibi has arthritis in her hands. She cannot use a manual tin opener because she has very poor grip. Her electric tin opener counts as an aid.

Francis was given an electric tin opener for Christmas. He has mobility problems, but no problems with his hands. Because he can use a manual tin opener, his electric one does not count as an aid to help him prepare food.

If you cannot cook on a hob because, for example, there is a risk of burns, but you can prepare the ingredients and then cook a meal using a microwave, you score two points. It is important to think about whether you are really safe when taking hot food out of a microwave – if you are not, you may score more points.

Also, if you can heat up ready meals but cannot prepare food to put in a microwave, you should explain why this is. You should be awarded a different descriptor for this activity, to reflect the help that you need to prepare food.

EXAMPLES

**Using a microwave**

Rose can put food in and out of her microwave safely. However, she can only heat up ready meals and tinned food, and cannot prepare fresh vegetables. She is assessed as needing assistance to prepare food.

Charlie is a widower. His wife used to do the cooking so most days he eats ready meals heated in a microwave. Unless there is a reason connected to Charlie's disability that means he cannot cook a meal, he will not score any points for this activity.

If you have mental health problems, you may need to be encouraged to cook proper meals by a friend or relative. It does not matter whether the other person has to come to your house, or just calls to remind and encourage you to make a meal. The important thing is that without this help you would not be able to prepare and cook a simple meal. For example, you might just eat takeaways and snacks as you cannot motivate yourself to cook.

If you cannot cook safely, you should be assessed as needing supervision when preparing or cooking food. For example, if you have epilepsy and do not get any warning of a seizure, you could be at risk of harm when chopping vegetables or handling hot food. If you are unable to understanding cooking instructions because you have an intellectual disability, then you may require supervision to keep you safe as you may burn food and be at risk of causing a fire.

If you cannot manage some cooking tasks reliably yourself (even using an aid), you could be assessed as needing physical assistance to prepare or cook food. If you have so many difficulties with preparing and cooking food that someone else needs to do all of the preparation and cooking for you, you should be assessed as being unable to prepare and cook food at all.

**EXAMPLE**

**Preparing food reliably**

Trish has obsessive compulsive disorder. She has no problem with the physical tasks needed to prepare food, but it takes her about four hours to prepare a simple meal by herself due to the amount of cleaning, organising and handwashing she does between each task.

Trish's husband encourages her to try to modify her routines to get food ready more quickly, but still has to do a lot of the cooking to get meals ready on time.

Trish cannot prepare and cook a meal within a reasonable time period and so is assessed as needing assistance to do so.

EXAMPLE

**Preparing food reliably**

Ella has chronic fatigue syndrome. On most days she can prepare herself some toast and a cup of tea. However, if she prepares and cooks a whole meal for herself from scratch, she is so exhausted that she ends up in bed for a couple of days. She therefore cannot prepare a simple meal as often as is reasonable.

If someone else helps Ella by doing some of the tasks, so she can prepare and cook meals reliably, she is assessed as needing assistance to prepare or cook a simple meal.

## 2. Do you have difficulty eating and drinking?

*What the law says*

**Activity two: taking nutrition**

| Descriptor | Points |
|---|---|
| (a) Can take nutrition unaided. | 0 |
| (b) Needs–<br>(i) to use an aid or appliance to be able to take nutrition; or<br>(ii) supervision to be able to take nutrition; or<br>(iii) assistance to be able to cut up food. | 2 |
| (c) Needs a therapeutic source to be able to take nutrition. | 2 |
| (d) Needs prompting to be able to take nutrition. | 4 |
| (e) Needs assistance to be able to manage a therapeutic source to take nutrition. | 6 |
| (f) Cannot convey food and drink to their mouth and needs another person to do so. | 10 |

*Schedule 1, Part 2 Social Security (Personal Independence Payment) Regulations 2013*

## What is looked at?

This 'activity' looks at how you eat and drink, including cutting up your food, chewing and swallowing it, and using a therapeutic source to gain nutrition. Dietary preferences, religious and cultural beliefs are not taken into account for this activity.

If you can eat independently but spill so much food that you need to change your clothes afterwards, this is not counted as eating to an acceptable standard and therefore you should score some points for this activity.

Aids that you might need include adapted cutlery or a specially designed cup with a drinking straw if you find it difficult to hold a cup or glass to your mouth without spilling its contents.

Box B

**Therapeutic source**

A 'therapeutic source' is defined as 'parenteral or enteral tube feeding, using a rate-limiting device such as a delivery system or feed pump'. This is when you are given food or drink through a tube going directly into either your intestines or your bloodstream, such as a peg feed or nasogastric tube (NG), or if you receive nutrition through an intravenous drip.

You score more points for this activity if you need help from someone else to use the equipment – for example, setting up a feeding tube.

If you are at risk of choking on food, but do not need to use a feeding tube to avoid the risk, you may be assessed as needing supervision to take nutrition, if the risk is serious enough.

If you do not eat an appropriate amount unless someone reminds or encourages you, you should be assessed as requiring prompting. This could be if your condition means that you overeat or if you would not eat proper meals without encouragement. You may need encouragement to cook a proper meal and also to eat it. These are two different needs, so you can score points for both this activity and the preparing food activity above.

The highest score for this activity is given if you need someone else to feed you and give you drinks – for example, if you are unable to use either of your arms.

**EXAMPLES**

**Assistance to manage a therapeutic source**

Rana uses a feeding pump that delivers nutrition to her overnight on a Monday and Friday. She cannot set up or put away the feeding pump herself due to her disabilities and requires assistance from another person.

Once the system has been set up, Rana requires no further help until the next morning.

As she requires help on the evening of one day and the morning of the next, Rana is counted as requiring assistance on most days in the week (Monday, Tuesday, Thursday and Friday) and should score six points for this activity.

**Prompting to eat**

Fritz has dementia, and often forgets to eat unless someone visits him and reminds him to have some food. Fritz needs prompting to eat.

Graham has a genetic disorder which means that he always feels hungry. He also has a learning disability and needs to be reminded to eat appropriate portions to manage his weight. Graham needs prompting to eat safely.

**Assistance to convey food and drink to your mouth**

Joy has motor neurone disease. She struggles to convey food and drink to her mouth due to the weakness in her arms and hands. She cannot do it on her own and requires her sister, who lives with Joy, to help her. If Joy was to try do it on her own, she would spill the food and drink and would not be able to eat much.

Joy needs another person to convey food and drink to her mouth.

## 3. Do you have difficulty taking medication, undergoing treatment at home, or keeping an eye on your health?

*What the law says*

**Activity three: managing therapy or monitoring a health condition**

| Descriptor | Points |
|---|---|
| (a) Either –<br>(i) does not receive medication or therapy or need to monitor a health condition; or<br>(ii) can manage medication or therapy or monitor a health condition unaided. | 0 |
| (b) Needs any one or more of the following –<br>(i) to use an aid or appliance to be able to manage medication;<br>(ii) supervision, prompting or assistance to be able to manage medication;<br>(iii) supervision, prompting or assistance to be able to monitor a health condition. | 1 |
| (c) Needs supervision, prompting or assistance to be able to manage therapy that takes no more than 3.5 hours a week. | 2 |
| (d) Needs supervision, prompting or assistance to be able to manage therapy that takes more than 3.5 but no more than seven hours a week. | 4 |
| (e) Needs supervision, prompting or assistance to be able to manage therapy that takes more than seven but no more than 14 hours a week. | 6 |
| (f) Needs supervision, prompting or assistance to be able to manage therapy that takes more than 14 hours a week. | 8 |

*Schedule 1, Part 2 Social Security (Personal Independence Payment) Regulations 2013*

**What is looked at?**

This 'activity' looks at the help you need with your medication or treatment at home, and whether you can detect changes in your condition which could be dangerous and take the necessary action. Only help that you need with medication taken or therapy carried out at home that has been prescribed or recommended by a doctor or other 'healthcare professional' counts.

An aid to help you take medication could be a special dosing pack that helps you take the right medicines at the right time, or a mobile phone alarm to remind you to take your tablets if you have memory problems. However, syringes, inhalers and nebulisers are not aids because they are the way you take medication and do not improve or replace physical or mental function. You may, however, score points if you require assistance from another person to use them.

If you are at risk of taking an overdose or you have epilepsy and may need emergency medication if you have a seizure, you may be assessed as needing supervision to manage your medication or monitor your health. If you cannot take your medicine without help from someone else, you also score points. This could apply if you cannot open a pill bottle or blister pack without help.

Box C

**Medication and therapy**

'Therapy' is anything to help with your condition that you have been told to do at home by your doctor or another healthcare professional, if your condition would worsen if you do not do it. You must need help with the therapy from another person to score points. Therapy does not include anything that could come under the medication descriptor instead.

Therapy includes:

- dialysis
- physiotherapy and specialist massages
- fitting bandages
- TENs machine therapy
- help to follow specialist diets

**EXAMPLE**

**Supervision to take medication**

Helen has severe depression and a history of suicide attempts. She needs supervision to take her medication, because she would be likely to take an overdose if someone was not there to check that she takes the right dose.

Although the assessment normally looks at your needs on different days, the therapy descriptors in this activity concern how long you need help during a week.

You are assessed as needing help with therapy on all the days in a week, irrespective of how the therapy is spread throughout the week. For example, if you need help with home dialysis, which you do three times a week, you are assessed as needing assistance with therapy on every day of a week in which you do the dialysis at home.

The periods of time mentioned refer to how long you need help for, not to how long your therapy takes overall. If you need help to set up a machine that is needed for your therapy, time someone else spends helping you with that also counts, even if you do not need any more help once the machine is set up.

**EXAMPLE**

**Help with therapy**

Imran had a stroke last year. He is regaining his speech and motor function slowly but has been told by his occupational therapist to do stretching exercises for half an hour a day and an hour of speech therapy. His partner helps with both of these.

Imran should be assessed as needing assistance with therapy for between seven and 14 hours a week, as long as his treatment is expected to last for at least a year.

**Note:** the DWP is looking again at some decisions made after 28 November 2016 which concern medication and monitoring, or diet as therapy. Get advice if you think you should have scored more points for this activity.

## 4. Do you have difficulty washing and bathing?

*What the law says*

**Activity four: washing and bathing**

| Descriptor | Points |
|---|---|
| (a) Can wash and bathe unaided. | 0 |
| (b) Needs to use an aid or appliance to be able to wash or bathe. | 2 |
| (c) Needs supervision or prompting to be able to wash or bathe. | 2 |
| (d) Needs assistance to be able to wash either their hair or body below the waist. | 2 |
| (e) Needs assistance to be able to get in or out of a bath or shower. | 3 |
| (f) Needs assistance to be able to wash their body between the shoulders and waist. | 4 |
| (g) Cannot wash and bathe at all and needs another person to wash their entire body. | 8 |

*Schedule 1, Part 2 Social Security (Personal Independence Payment) Regulations 2013*

### What is looked at?

This 'activity' looks at the help you need to keep clean by washing. Most of the descriptors focus on having a bath or shower.

Aids that you might need to use include a bath lift, a shower seat or grab rails in the shower. If you have mental health problems and need to be encouraged to keep yourself clean, you should score points for this activity if someone has to prompt you to have a shower. It is arguable you still may require prompting even if you can sometimes complete the activity without this help – for example, if you can wash on a day you have something important to do.

If you need someone to keep an eye on you while you are in the bath or shower (for example, because you are at risk of falls or have uncontrolled epilepsy), you may be assessed as needing supervision to bathe. You should not be expected to reduce the amount of time you wash or bathe to avoid risk.

If you have to remove your hearing aid or cochlear implant processor to shower or bathe and therefore would not be able to hear a standard fire or smoke alarm, or hear someone breaking into your home, this means you require an aid or appliance, or supervision or prompting. **Note:** the DWP is looking again at some decisions made after 21 August 2020 which concern this. Get advice if you think you should have scored more points for this activity.

To wash to an acceptable standard, you should be clean when you finish. Even if you can reach an area such as your feet, this does not necessarily mean you can wash them properly. If it takes you a long time to wash without help, you arguably require assistance to do so.

If you would need help from someone else to get into an unadapted bath, you should score points for needing assistance to do so, even if you actually have a wet room or grab rails fitted that mean you manage at home without anyone else to help you.

**EXAMPLES**

**Washing and bathing**

Neil is autistic. He can wash himself, but is obsessed with water and so stays in the bath for hours unless encouraged to get out by his support worker. He needs prompting to be able to bathe in a reasonable time.

Kerry finds it hard to wash her legs as she has trouble bending down due to back problems. Her husband normally helps her to do this. She needs assistance to wash her body below the waist.

## 5. Do you have difficulty using the toilet?

*What the law says*

**Activity five: managing toilet needs or incontinence**

| Descriptor | Points |
|---|---|
| (a) Can manage toilet needs or incontinence unaided. | 0 |
| (b) Needs to use an aid or appliance to be able to manage toilet needs or incontinence. | 2 |
| (c) Needs supervision or prompting to be able to manage toilet needs. | 2 |
| (d) Needs assistance to be able to manage toilet needs. | 4 |
| (e) Needs assistance to be able to manage incontinence of either bladder or bowel. | 6 |
| (f) Needs assistance to be able to manage incontinence of both bladder and bowel. | 8 |

*Schedule 1, Part 2 Social Security (Personal Independence Payment) Regulations 2013*

### What is looked at?

Box D

**Toilet needs and managing incontinence**

This 'activity' looks at very specific areas in which you might need help. 'Toilet needs' means:

- getting on and off an unadapted toilet
- using the toilet
- cleaning yourself afterwards

Even if you only need an aid or help from someone else with one of these three aspects, you should still score some points.

'Manage incontinence' means to deal with continence problems of the bladder or bowel, including using a collecting device like a pad or catheter, and to clean yourself afterwards.

Any other difficulties, such as undressing to go to the toilet or mobilising to get to the toilet, are not considered.

A commode may count as an aid, but only if you need it due to incontinence problems, and not if you use it as you need help to get upstairs to your bathroom. Other examples of aids to manage your toilet needs may include a bidet or shower head if you find it hard to clean yourself, or a raised toilet seat or grab rails to help you use the toilet safely.

Incontinence pads and stomas or catheters are examples of aids to help with continence. If it is reasonable for you to use incontinence pads for the majority of the time as a precaution, you still can score points for requiring an aid or appliance, even if you are not actually incontinent on all these days.

You score more points if you need physical help from another person – for example, with wiping yourself or getting up from the toilet. If you use a catheter or a collecting bag and need help with this from another person, you are assessed as needing help with managing incontinence.

You score more points if you need help with incontinence of both your bladder and bowel.

EXAMPLE

**Managing toilet needs and incontinence**

Marta uses a colostomy bag since having part of her colon removed. She does not need help using it, so is assessed as needing an aid or appliance to manage her toilet needs.

A few years later, Marta develops problems with her hands and cannot empty the bag without help. She tells the DWP about this and is reassessed as needing assistance to manage incontinence.

Ellie has Crohn's disease. Due to the unpredictability of her condition, Ellie wears incontinence pads every day to mitigate any flare-ups. This is reasonable use of pads and therefore Ellie will be assessed as requiring an aid or appliance to manage her incontinence.

EXAMPLE

**Bladder and bowel incontinence**

Jonah has multiple sclerosis which has caused permanent bladder and bowel incontinence. He works as a self-employed window cleaner. Jonah has aids in the back of his van, specifically a bucket and cleaning material, to enable him to clean himself after being incontinent. It takes him around 10 minutes to clean himself properly. He cannot complete the activity within a reasonable time and would need assistance from another person to be able to. He therefore scores 8 points under descriptor (f).

## 6. Do you have difficulty getting dressed or undressed?

*What the law says*

**Activity six: dressing and undressing**

| Descriptor | Points |
|---|---|
| (a) Can dress and undress unaided. | 0 |
| (b) Needs to use an aid or appliance to be able to dress or undress. | 2 |
| (c) Needs either–<br>(i) prompting to be able to dress, undress or determine appropriate circumstances for remaining clothed; or<br>(ii) prompting or assistance to be able to select appropriate clothing. | 2 |
| (d) Needs assistance to be able to dress or undress their lower body. | 2 |
| (e) Needs assistance to be able to dress or undress their upper body. | 4 |
| (f) Cannot dress or undress at all. | 8 |

*Schedule 1, Part 2 Social Security (Personal Independence Payment) Regulations 2013*

### What is looked at?

This 'activity' considers getting dressed or undressed. You do not need to have difficulties with both dressing and undressing to score points.

Aids for this activity include things to help you dress, such as grabbers for your socks and a long shoe horn.

If you have to wear clothing that makes it easier to dress without help, such as velcro fastenings, large buttons, front-fastening bras, zips and loose-fitting clothing, this counts as an aid if you need it because of your health condition or disability, but not if you just prefer to wear these kind of clothes.

If you must sit down to dress or undress, this does not count as needing an aid or appliance; however, it may indicate other help is required.

You may need someone to tell you what to wear. For example, this might be because you have a visual impairment and cannot see whether clothes are dirty, or because you have a learning disability and do not remember to dress warmly in winter.

You may also need someone to tell you when to dress and undress because you may have a cognitive impairment meaning you are likely to undress in public.

If you take a long time to choose clothes because it is traumatic due to a condition such as body dysmorphia, then you may score points for requiring prompting.

Your ability to put on or take off shoes and socks is also considered. If you need help to get your shoes on, that counts as assistance with dressing the lower body.

You score more points if you need help to dress your upper body. If someone has to help you put on all your clothes, you are assessed as being unable to dress at all.

EXAMPLE

**Dressing and undressing**

Nadja is registered blind. She can dress herself but needs someone to tell her whether her clothes are clean, so she is assessed as needing prompting to dress.

After being awarded PIP, she has a stroke and this leaves her left arm and leg almost completely paralysed. She is very determined and can still dress herself, but this takes her almost an hour if there is no one to help her. This is more than twice as long as someone without her condition may take to get dressed, meaning Nadja is counted as unable to dress within a reasonable time period. She therefore scores points for needing assistance to dress, even though she does not currently get this.

## 7. Do you have difficulty speaking and hearing?

*What the law says*

**Activity seven: communicating verbally**

| Descriptor | Points |
|---|---|
| (a) Can express and understand verbal information unaided. | 0 |
| (b) Needs to use an aid or appliance to be able to speak or hear. | 2 |
| (c) Needs communication support to be able to express or understand complex verbal information. | 4 |
| (d) Needs communication support to be able to express or understand basic verbal information. | 8 |
| (e) Cannot express or understand verbal information at all even with communication support. | 12 |

*Schedule 1, Part 2 Social Security (Personal Independence Payment) Regulations 2013*

### What is looked at?

This 'activity' looks at your ability to speak and hear. It introduces a different type of help that someone may require and does not include points for prompting, supervision or assistance. If your first language is not English, you are assessed on how you communicate in your first language.

Aids that might help you to speak or hear can include hearing aids or an electronic voice aid if you are unable to speak.

Box E

**Verbal information and communication support**

'Basic verbal information' means a simple sentence in your native language. For example, 'I need the toilet'.

'Complex verbal information' means more than one sentence or a more complicated sentence in your native language. For example, 'I need the toilet. I have tried to find them but can't. Do you know where they are?'

Communication support is support from another person trained or experienced in communicating with people with specific communication needs. This could be a professional, but is more likely to be a close friend or family member who understands your speech well.

Your ability to read, write or send text messages is not usually considered, but if you cannot speak and use writing to communicate, then this could be an aid.

Any ability to lip read is disregarded for this activity, so you can still score points.

If you suffer from a condition like anxiety, which affects your ability to speak, hear or understand in certain social situations, you are unlikely to score points for this activity. You are more likely to score points for difficulties engaging with other people (Activity nine).

You are awarded the most points if you cannot communicate verbally at all, even with support from someone who knows you well.

EXAMPLES

**Communicating verbally**

Andrew has been profoundly deaf since birth. He cannot speak at all, but is fluent in British Sign Language. He is assessed as needing communication support to express basic verbal information.

Selena has had multiple strokes and struggles with her speech. She can understand what people are saying to her, but they cannot understand what she is saying to them.

Her daughter, Gabby, is experienced in communicating with Selena and is really the only person who can understand what Selena is saying.

Gabby therefore provides communication support whenever it is needed and with all speech. Selena is assessed as needing communication support to express basic verbal information.

EXAMPLE

**Needing an aid to speak**

Petra had her larynx removed after being diagnosed with throat cancer. She uses an electronic voice aid, which means strangers can understand her speech. She is assessed as needing an aid to speak.

## 8. Do you have difficulty reading?

*What the law says*

**Activity eight: reading and understanding signs, symbols and words**

| Descriptor | Points |
|---|---|
| (a) Can read and understand basic and complex written information either unaided or using spectacles or contact lenses. | 0 |
| (b) Needs to use an aid or appliance, other than spectacles or contact lenses, to be able to read or understand either basic or complex written information. | 2 |
| (c) Needs prompting to be able to read or understand complex written information. | 2 |
| (d) Needs prompting to be able to read or understand basic written information. | 4 |
| (e) Cannot read or understand signs, symbols or words at all. | 8 |

*Schedule 1, Part 2 Social Security (Personal Independence Payment) Regulations 2013*

### What is looked at?

This 'activity' looks at the problems you have reading. If you cannot read English, but can read another language without any problems, you score no points. If you need to use glasses or contact lenses to read but have no other problems reading, you score no points. If you only have an issue with one eye, but your other is fine, you score no points. If you can only read Braille, you are assessed as unable to read at all. If you never learned to read, then you score no points unless this is directly linked to a physical or mental condition.

Aids that you may need to help you read could include a magnifying glass or a letter reader that magnifies text. When deciding how many points you score, your ability to read using aids like these both inside and outside your home is considered. This means that you may be able to score points for this activity if you only have problems in the dark or very bright light, depending on how serious your problems reading in these conditions are and how often you are affected.

EXAMPLE

**Reading with an aid**

Roxanne is partially sighted and uses a specialist magnifier at home to understand the content of letters. The DWP assesses her as needing an aid or appliance to read, because it decides she could use a magnifying glass when out of the house. She asks for the decision to be looked at again and explains that her vision is so poor that she cannot use a magnifying glass for bus timetables or labels on items in shops. The DWP agrees and changes her award to descriptor 8(c).

If you can read words, but do not understand the information and need someone to explain what it means, you score points in this activity. You score more points if you need help understanding 'basic written information'. If you can understand these things but need help with reading sentences, you are assessed as needing help to understand 'complex written information'. Note that the standard of reading required is low.

BOX F

**Basic and complex written information**

'Basic written information' means signs, symbols and dates written or printed as standard size text in your native language – for example, the ability to read a few words, used to convey a message, on a street sign.

'Complex written information' is more than one sentence of written or printed standard size text in your native language – for example, reading a short appointment letter.

**EXAMPLES**

**Help with reading**

Sebastian has Down's syndrome. He can read very simple sentences if someone explains what some of the words mean, but needs prompting to understand letters or recipes. He is assessed as needing help to understand complex written information.

Tina is registered blind. She is an academic and author of several books. However, as she has completely lost her sight and can only read Braille, she is assessed as unable to read.

## 9. Do you have difficulty mixing with other people?

*What the law says*

**Activity nine: engaging with other people face to face**

| Descriptor | Points |
|---|---|
| (a) Can engage with other people unaided. | 0 |
| (b) Needs prompting to be able to engage with other people. | 2 |
| (c) Needs social support to be able to engage with other people. | 4 |
| (d) Cannot engage with other people due to such engagement causing either – (i) overwhelming psychological distress to the claimant; or (ii) the claimant to exhibit behaviour which would result in a substantial risk of harm to the claimant or another person. | 8 |

*Schedule 1, Part 2 Social Security (Personal Independence Payment) Regulations 2013*

### What is looked at?

This 'activity' looks at whether you can behave appropriately in social situations, understand other people's body language and feelings, and form relationships. Some people are less comfortable in social situations than others. To score points for this activity, your problems with social interaction must be caused by a physical or mental condition, rather than your personal preference. It may be that a physical health problem (such as continence problems or a severe skin condition) makes you worried about meeting other people. If this makes you so severely anxious that you are considered to have anxiety as a mental health condition, and need help from another person to meet others, you should score some points for this activity. Like Activity seven, this activity introduces another type of help from another person, social support, and does not include points for supervision or assistance.

Box G
**Social support**

'Social support' means support from a person trained or experienced in helping people to engage in a social setting. It is not necessary for the person providing social support to always be with you; the support can be given before, during or after the social interaction. What is important is that the support you get allows you to engage with other people, and you would not be able to do so without that help. If you normally get help from a family member who knows you very well, for this to be social support there must be a reason that encouragement from someone you do not know well would not allow you to engage with other people.

If you need some extra help, but not necessarily from a professional or someone who knows you very well, you are assessed as needing 'prompting' rather than social support, and you score fewer points for this activity.

Engaging specifically includes establishing relationships. This means you must be able to engage further than just responding to questions. You may still score points if you can engage in very specific circumstances or social settings without help, but your condition would prevent you from engaging in all types of settings.

You must also be able to engage with all types of people. For example, if you can engage with the same gender with no difficulties, but cannot engage with another gender due to your condition, then the fact you can engage with that specific group of people is disregarded.

EXAMPLES

**Social support and prompting**

Zohar has anxiety and severe depression. She has lost touch with most of her friends, and only feels comfortable around her closest friend and her sister. She is able to spend some time with other people she knows less well, but only if her closest friend or sister is there to support her. Her sister and closest friend have got used to helping her manage over the past couple of years. Even though neither has any formal training, Zohar is assessed as needing social support to engage with other people.

Violet also has depression. Her friends noticed that she was not turning up when they had arranged to meet. They now make sure that someone calls Violet a few hours beforehand to encourage her to come along, and this means that Violet is able to stay in touch and is much less isolated. Violet needs prompting to engage with other people.

If you are not normally able to interact with others, even with the help of a relative or a professional, you score more points. Your problems must be due to how upset you get by this, or there being a risk of harm to you or someone else as a result of your behaviour around other people. Overwhelming 'psychological distress' means distress relating to a mental health condition or an intellectual or cognitive impairment – for example, panic attacks, fatigue, aggression and anxiety attacks.

EXAMPLE

**Establishing a relationship**

Sajid has severe mental health needs and cannot engage with other people without his partner who has been supporting him for over 20 years. Sajid can, however, go to the pub four times a week. He goes into the pub, orders a drink, then sits in the corner and does not speak to anyone. Even though he can complete this seemingly social activity, he does not engage further than ordering a drink. He therefore requires social support to engage with others.

**Note:** the DWP's definition of social support used to be less generous, so it is contacting people who had a PIP decision after 6 April 2016 to look at their claims again. Get advice if you need social support and think you should have scored points for this activity.

## 10. Do you have difficulty managing money?

*What the law says*

**Activity 10: making budgeting decisions**

| Descriptor | Points |
|---|---|
| (a) Can manage complex budgeting decisions unaided. | 0 |
| (b) Needs prompting or assistance to be able to make complex budgeting decisions. | 2 |
| (c) Needs prompting or assistance to be able to make simple budgeting decisions. | 4 |
| (d) Cannot make any budgeting decisions at all. | 6 |

*Schedule 1, Part 2 Social Security (Personal Independence Payment) Regulations 2013*

### What is looked at?

This 'activity' looks at your ability to manage money. Your difficulty with this activity must be due to your health conditions and not because you have poor money management skills. It is unlikely you will score points if your difficulties are solely due to a physical condition; however, you may score points if you suffer with a visual impairment.

You are assessed as needing help with 'complex budgeting decisions' if someone needs to help you manage your household bills. If you need help to work out simple sums, such as how much change you should be given in a shop, or adding together the prices of things to work out how much money you need, you are assessed as needing help with 'simple budgeting decisions'.

If, because of a disability or health condition, you cannot add or subtract or you do not understand the value of money, you are assessed as being unable to make budgeting decisions at all.

**EXAMPLES**

**Making budgeting decisions**

Ildiko has bipolar disorder. Although she was very good at maths at school, when she is having a manic episode she often erratically spends all her money on large and inappropriate presents, and then does not have anything left for her bills or to buy food. If she is feeling low, she ignores the bills unless her brother encourages her to pay them.

Ildiko is assessed as needing prompting to make complex budgeting decisions.

Conrad has a learning disability. He can do simple addition, but often needs to be reminded to think about how much money he has by his support worker when they are shopping, and cannot calculate change.

Conrad is assessed as needing prompting to make simple budgeting decisions.

## Further information

CPAG's *Welfare Benefits Handbook* contains detailed information about the PIP daily living activities, with references to the legislation and the most important caselaw.

There are various resources on gov.uk that help to explain how the DWP interprets the daily living activities and decides which descriptors you satisfy. These include Chapter P2 of *Advice for Decision Making*, the *PIP Assessment Guide part 2: the assessment criteria* and the *PIP Handbook*.

Disability Rights UK has produced a useful guide on claiming PIP, with information about how to explain your problems with the different daily living activities on the assessment questionnaire. You can download it at disabilityrightsuk.org/personal-independence-payment-pip.

Rightsnet produces the website pipinfo.net, which gives further explanations of the terms within the descriptors, along with helpful information relating to specific conditions and how you may meet certain descriptors.

# Chapter 6
# The mobility activities

This chapter covers:

1. Do you have difficulty planning or following journeys?
2. Do you have difficulty walking?

## What you need to know

- There are two mobility 'activities' in the personal independence payment (PIP) assessment.
- Each activity contains a series of statements (called 'descriptors') which score a certain number of points.
- If you score at least eight points in total, you are awarded the 'mobility component', paid at the standard rate. If you score 12 points or more in total, you are awarded the enhanced rate.
- Only the activities explained in this chapter are taken into account. Any other help you need is not counted.

## 1. Do you have difficulty planning or following journeys?

### What is looked at?

This 'activity' looks at your ability to work out and follow the route of a journey. If you need encouragement to go out or cannot go out at all most days, you also score points for this activity.

When considering which points you score, the entire journey should be assessed.

*What the law says*

**Activity one: planning and following journeys**

| Descriptor | Points |
|---|---|
| (a) Can plan and follow the route of a journey unaided. | 0 |
| (b) Needs prompting to be able to undertake any journey to avoid overwhelming psychological distress to the claimant. | 4 |
| (c) Cannot plan the route of a journey. | 8 |
| (d) Cannot follow the route of an unfamiliar journey without another person, assistance dog or orientation aid. | 10 |
| (e) Cannot undertake any journey because it would cause overwhelming psychological distress to the claimant. | 10 |
| (f) Cannot follow the route of a familiar journey without another person, an assistance dog or an orientation aid. | 12 |

*Schedule 1, Part 3 Social Security (Personal Independence Payment) Regulations 2013*

For example, if you can drive to a destination without any issues, the DWP must also consider how you manage leaving the house, walking to the car, getting in the car, exiting the car and then walking to your destination point, such as into a building.

If you cannot complete the whole journey without support, then you are counted as unable to complete the activity.

Short and specific journeys can be disregarded. For example, you may be able to walk to a specific shop at the end of your road without support because it is not far and you are used to the journey, but you would not be able to manage any other journey.

Box A

**Help to follow journeys**

An 'assistance dog' is a dog trained to guide or assist a person with a sensory impairment.

'Orientation aids' are specialist aids designed to assist disabled people following a route, such as a long white cane. If you use something like a smartphone app to help you, whether it counts as an orientation aid or not depends on whether it is designed to help someone with your condition or not. A sat nav is not an orientation aid.

There is no definition of another person, but the other person must be helping you to follow the route – ie, to navigate the path of your journey.

'Prompting' is someone reminding or encouraging you to go out, even if they only do this by phone. However, the help must be needed to get you out of the house.

Box B

**Psychological distress**

'Psychological distress' means distress related to a mental health condition or an intellectual or cognitive impairment. Your mental health condition may have an underlying physical cause. For example, you may have unmanageable incontinence which means you are anxious about making journeys outside the home. If this anxiety is significant enough to be recognised as a separate mental condition, and is so severe that you cannot go out on most days, you score sufficient points to qualify for the standard rate of the 'mobility component'. Psychological distress could include fatigue, aggression and anxiety attacks.

You can only satisfy descriptors 1(d) and 1(f) due to anxiety if you need someone with you to avoid *overwhelming* psychological distress. That person does not need to be taking action to help you if their presence alone is enough to relieve the distress.

Unexpected changes to the environment, such as roadworks and changed bus stops, are commonplace problems with navigating that you may encounter, so think about whether you could manage if such disruption occurred. If you could not manage to find an alternative route without help, you should be assessed as needing help from another person to follow the route of a journey. How many points you score depends on whether you would have problems with all journeys, or just unfamiliar ones.

If you cannot plan the route of a journey (for example, due to a cognitive impairment), you qualify for the standard rate of the mobility component even if you could follow a journey that someone else has planned for you without any problems.

**Note:** the DWP is contacting claimants who get PIP (or have been refused it since 28 November 2016) who might score more points for this activity. Get advice if you if you think the effects of psychological distress were not taken into account and you think you should have scored more points for this activity or been entitled to PIP.

EXAMPLES

**Planning and following journeys**

Lukas has anxiety and depression. Due to his mental health problems, he does not go out at all most days, even if someone comes round and offers to go out with him. He is assessed as being unable to undertake any journey. He scores 10 points and gets the standard rate mobility component.

Veronique has a visual impairment. She uses a white cane whenever she is out, including to get to her local shops or pick up her children from their primary school. She is assessed as needing an orientation aid to follow a familiar journey. She scores 12 points and is entitled to the enhanced rate mobility component.

## 2. Do you have difficulty walking?

*What the law says*

**Activity two: moving around**

| Descriptor | Points |
|---|---|
| (a) Can stand and then move more than 200 metres, either aided or unaided. | 0 |
| (b) Can stand and then move more than 50 metres but no more than 200 metres, either aided or unaided. | 4 |
| (c) Can stand and then move unaided more than 20 metres but no more than 50 metres. | 8 |
| (d) Can stand and then move using an aid or appliance more than 20 metres but no more than 50 metres. | 10 |
| (e) Can stand and then move more than one metre but no more than 20 metres, either aided or unaided. | 12 |
| (f) Cannot, either aided or unaided, (i) stand; or (ii) move more than one metre. | 12 |

*Schedule 1, Part 3 Social Security (Personal Independence Payment) Regulations 2013*

### What is looked at?

This 'activity' looks at your ability to walk without severe discomfort, such as breathlessness, pain or fatigue. It distinguishes between your ability to stand and then walk up to 20 metres, up to 50 metres, up to 200 metres and more than 200 metres.

It is often hard to work out how many metres you can move. It may be helpful to know that a double decker bus is around 10 metres long and a standard swimming pool is 25 metres long.

Box C

**Aided/unaided and standing**

'Aided' means either that you use an aid, such as crutches, a walking stick or a prosthetic limb, or that another person helps you to walk.

'Stand' is defined as standing upright with at least one biological foot on the ground, with or without suitable aids. A prosthetic leg is considered an aid, so if you have had some or all of one leg amputated, you are considered able to stand. If you have had both legs amputated, you are assessed as unable to stand.

'Stand and then move' means to be able to stand and then move independently while remaining standing. Any movement you make using a wheelchair is ignored, as this is not included in the definition of 'stand and then move'.

When you are working out the distance you can manage, remember that the assessment looks at what you can manage 'reliably'. This means safely, to an acceptable standard, repeatedly and in a reasonable time period. So you should think about the manner in which you are able to walk: your gait, your speed, the risk of falls and any symptoms or side effects that could affect your ability to walk any distance, such as pain, breathlessness and fatigue. If moving causes you pain, you can still score points for this activity, even if the cause of the pain is not diagnosed. If your difficulties are caused by psychological distress, you will not score points for this activity and likely will score points for mobility Activity one instead.

Your ability to walk is judged on the type of surface you would normally expect outdoors, such as pavements and whether or not you can manage kerbs. Remember, it is your ability to walk on flat ground, rather than uneven ground, stairs or steep slopes, that is assessed.

If you can manage more that 50 metres using an aid or appliance or with help, you are unlikely to satisfy descriptor 2(c), even if you can only manage less than 50 metres unaided.

EXAMPLES

**Moving around**

Harbajhan has chronic obstructive pulmonary disease. He can walk about 50 metres before needing a break and then manage that distance again a few more times most days, but after the first 25 metres or so he gets extreme shortness of breath and pain in his chest. He is assessed as being able to stand and then move unaided more than 20 metres, but no more than 50 metres. He scores eight points and is entitled to the standard rate 'mobility component'.

Ava has advanced multiple sclerosis. She can stand from her bed and go to the bathroom next door using a walking frame, but cannot go any further without transferring to a wheelchair. She is assessed as being able to move more than one metre but no more than 20 metres, either aided or unaided. She scores 12 points and is entitled to the enhanced rate mobility component.

Sophie has emphysema and gets out of breath after about 150 metres if she tries to walk too quickly. However, if she paces herself, she can walk over a mile, taking a short pause every 400 metres or so. She is assessed as able to walk over 200 metres reliably. She scores no points for the moving around activity.

## *Further information*

CPAG's *Welfare Benefits Handbook* contains detailed information about the PIP mobility activities, with references to the legislation and the most important caselaw.

There are various resources on gov.uk that help to explain how the DWP interprets the mobility activities and decides which descriptors you satisfy. These include Chapter P2 of *Advice for Decision Making*, the *PIP Assessment Guide part 2: the assessment criteria* and the *PIP Handbook*.

Disability Rights UK has produced a useful guide on claiming PIP, with information about how to explain your problems with the different mobility activities on the assessment questionnaire. You can download it at disabilityrightsuk.org/personal-independence-payment-pip.

Rightsnet produces the website pipinfo.net, which gives futher explanations of the terms within the descriptors, along with helpful information relating to specific conditions and how you may meet certain descriptors.

# Chapter 7
# Challenging and changing decisions

**This chapter covers:**

1. What can you do if you disagree with a decision?
2. What happens if your circumstances change?

**What you need to know**

- If you disagree with a decision on your personal independence payment (PIP) claim, you can challenge it.
- You must first ask the DWP for a 'mandatory reconsideration'.
- If you are still unhappy after the mandatory reconsideration, you can appeal to an independent tribunal.
- If your health condition or disability gets worse, you should notify the DWP so your entitlement can be reviewed. You may be entitled to a higher amount of PIP.

## 1. What can you do if you disagree with a decision?

If you disagree with a decision, you can challenge it. You must first ask for a 'mandatory reconsideration' (the law refers to this as requesting a 'revision' of the decision).

If you are still unhappy, you can appeal.

*What CPAG says*

**Challenging a decision when you already have an award**

When you challenge a PIP decision, the DWP and, if relevant, the appeal tribunal can look at your whole award again. This means that if you already have a PIP award, you could risk ending up with a lower award or losing your award altogether. It could be useful to get advice from a Citizens Advice or other welfare rights service before asking for a mandatory reconsideration. You can find free advice services using advicelocal.uk.

EXAMPLE

**Challenging a decision: potential risk**

Sue has claimed PIP and been awarded the enhanced rate 'mobility component' but nothing for daily living. She wants to challenge the decision as she believes she should be entitled to at least the standard 'daily living component'. She is worried about the potential risk to her award as the enhanced rate mobility component gives her access to the Motability scheme, which is important to her. She decides to seek advice before challenging the decision.

### How do you ask for a mandatory reconsideration?

When the DWP makes a decision on your claim for PIP, it must let you know this in writing. This letter is called a 'decision notice' and will explain the decision that has been made, including brief details why. If you disagree with the decision, you can request a mandatory reconsideration. You can also ask for a further explanation of the decision by phoning the DWP on the number provided, or a copy of the 'healthcare professional' report, but you do not have to do this before requesting a mandatory reconsideration. You can request a mandatory reconsideration in writing or by phone. The DWP should treat any request to look at the decision again as a mandatory reconsideration request; however, it is helpful to clearly state that you are requesting a mandatory reconsideration, to ensure it is done.

Try to give a full explanation of why you think the decision is wrong by, for example, explaining where you think you should have scored sufficient points in the assessment. If you make your request by phone, you may wish to state brief reasons and then send a written document further explaining the reasoning and including evidence. It is a good idea to get free benefits advice to help you with this. There is also a mandatory reconsideration form (Form MR1) that you can find on gov.uk, but it may be better to structure the request yourself.

You should try to ask for a mandatory reconsideration within one month of the date of the decision. This is the date on the letter the DWP sends you. You can ask for a mandatory reconsideration late as long as the request is within 13 months of the date of the decision and you have 'good reason' for lateness. 'Good reason' could be because you have been in hospital and unable to make the request, or you have been waiting for help from an advice service and they had no immediate appointments. You must identify the good reason when you make the late request.

EXAMPLE

**Time limit**

Steve has anxiety and agoraphobia. He applies for PIP, but is turned down for both components. He relies on his daughter to help him deal with his post and she is away on holiday when the decision notice arrives. By the time she is back, the one-month deadline for challenging the decision has passed. With the help of his daughter, Steve writes a letter to the DWP asking for a late mandatory reconsideration. In the letter he explains why he disagrees with the decision and also why he was not able to meet the deadline. His daughter includes a note and a copy of her flight confirmations to support this. Steve also attaches a copy of a letter from his psychiatrist, confirming his difficulties, which he did not have when he first applied.

The DWP can, however rarely does, refuse a request for a late mandatory reconsideration. If it does refuse, you are still able to appeal to the tribunal, providing proof of the DWP's refusal.

The more information you can supply to support your case, the better the chance you have of getting the decision changed. In particular, make sure you send any further evidence you have from your GP, hospital specialist or other health professional who supports your claim. If you are waiting for further evidence, do not delay making your mandatory reconsideration request. You can make the request and inform the DWP that evidence will be sent seperately.

Someone from the DWP may phone you to ask for further information about why you disagree with the decision. It may be helpful if you can provide further information, but do not feel pressured into agreeing with parts of the decision that you think are wrong. At the end of the call, you should be very clear that you still want your mandatory reconsideration request to be considered.

The DWP looks at your arguments and any further evidence you send, and then issues you with a 'mandatory reconsideration notice' telling you whether or not the decision has been changed and brief reasons why. If the decision is changed and you are awarded a higher rate of PIP, you usually receive that amount from your claim date (usually the date you phoned to make the initial claim), which means you receive a lump sum then the higher rate going forward. If you receive a lump sum, it is disregarded from means-tested benefits like universal credit for 12 months.

*What CPAG says*

**Mandatory reconsiderations**

CPAG suggests that:

- even if you request a mandatory reconsideration by phone, you confirm it in writing as well
- if the DWP phones you, be very clear at the end of the call that you still want your request to be considered
- if someone is helping you to challenge the decision, you could ask the DWP to phone them instead

**How do you appeal?**

If a mandatory reconsideration has been completed and you are still unhappy, you can appeal to a tribunal, which is independent of the DWP.

You should appeal to the tribunal within one month of the date on your mandatory reconsideration notice. This time limit can be extended by up to 12 months if special circumstances prevented you from appealing within a month. It is best to appeal before the month's deadline if you can, because it can be harder to make a late appeal.

The easiest and quickest way to submit an appeal is by completing the online Form SSCS1 at gov.uk/appeal-benefit-decision/submit-appeal. You can upload documents directly to the online form, or send them later via email or post.

You also could use a paper Form SSCS1, available to download from gov.uk. Send this form directly to HM Courts and Tribunals Service, not to the DWP.

Even if you do not have Form SSCS1 and cannot make an online submission, do not delay making your appeal. Write to HM Courts and Tribunals Service and include all the information and documents listed in Box A below. The address for HM Courts and Tribunals Service is HMCTS SSCS Benefits Appeals, PO Box 12626, Harlow CM20 9QF.

You can choose either to attend a hearing of your appeal (this is called an oral hearing) or have it decided 'on the papers'. If you choose for your appeal to be decided 'on the papers', you do not attend a hearing and the decision is based on the written information that you and the DWP provide. An oral hearing may be face to face, by telephone or via video call.

If you choose to attend a hearing, the tribunal panel has the opportunity to ask you questions in person (but cannot perform a medical examination). The panel usually comprises three members: a legal member who knows how to apply legislation (ie, a judge), a medical member who can understand your health conditions (eg, a doctor) and a disability specialist who understands the difficulties disabled people may face (eg, a carer).

Box A

**Appeal checklist**

Your appeal must be signed and include:

- a copy of your mandatory reconsideration notice (for the online form, just the date of the notice)
- your name and address
- your national insurance number
- the address where documents relating to your appeal can be sent or delivered (usually either your own address or that of your representative if you have one)
- the reasons why you think the decision is wrong – give as much detail as you can about why the decision is wrong, such as where you think you should have scored points in the assessment
- whether or not you want to attend a hearing of your appeal
- if your appeal is outside the one-month time limit, an explanation of why it is late
- the name and address of your representative if you have one; this authorises HM Courts and Tribunals Service to deal with that person about your appeal, and they should be sent copies of your appeal paperwork

*What CPAG says*

**Appeal hearings**

Statistics show that you have a much greater chance of success if you attend an appeal hearing. This can be an intimidating idea, but if you can get a representative, or even a friend or relative, to accompany you, this may help to make the experience less stressful.

Remember, the tribunal panel is independent of the DWP and will thoroughly listen to all information provided to make a decision.

In some cases, if the tribunal thinks you are highly likely to win your appeal, it may consider your appeal at what is known as a 'triage session'. If it thinks your appeal could be decided without a hearing, it can make a provisional decision and notify you and the DWP. If you are offered a provisional decision, seek advice. If you or the DWP still want an oral hearing, however, one must take place.

You do not have to have a representative, but it can be a good idea. The appeal process can be confusing and stressful, and your chances of success are generally better if you have an expert to help you. This could be an adviser from a Citizens Advice or other benefits advice service, or a friend or relative who has good knowledge of benefits matters. Representatives can also ease some of the stress of an appeal by receiving documents from the DWP or HM Courts and Tribunals Service, and submitting evidence on your behalf.

Once HM Court and Tribunals Service receives your SSCS1 form (that day, if submitting the online form) or appeal letter, it notifies the DWP, which then has 28 days to respond. The DWP response is called the 'appeal papers' or sometimes the 'bundle'. It is sent to you and your representative if you have one. It includes all information regarding your PIP claim including a copy of your claim form, the healthcare professional report, the reasons for the decision, mandatory reconsideration information, supporting evidence you have already provided, and any relevant law on which the DWP is relying. There could also be information regarding previous PIP decisions, disability living allowance decisions or relevant work capability assessments (either from employment and support allowance or universal credit).

You should thoroughly read the appeal papers and then put together a written argument (or 'submission') for the tribunal based on the information and argument the DWP provides. You can ask your representative or a benefits adviser to help with this.

Once the hearing has happened, you will receive a notice from the tribunal containing the decision. If you are awarded a higher rate of PIP, then your award usually increases from your claim date, meaning you receive a lump sum and the higher rate going forward.

If you receive a means-tested benefit such as universal credit, then this lump sum is disregarded for 12 months.

If you disagree with the tribunal's decision, you can only appeal it in very specific circumstances. Get advice as soon as possible if you disagree with how the tribunal made its decision.

EXAMPLE

**Appeals**

Steve's late request for a mandatory reconsideration is accepted, but when he receives his mandatory reconsideration notice it says that the decision has not been changed and that he is still not entitled to any PIP.

He decides to appeal and approaches a local welfare rights service for help. An adviser helps him complete Form SSCS1 and agrees to be his representative.

Steve chooses to attend a hearing, and the representative arranges a taxi to the hearing and makes sure Steve's daughter is free to accompany him. At the hearing, Steve gives a full explanation of the help he needs, and he is awarded the PIP mobility component.

## 2. What happens if your circumstances change?

If you are getting PIP and your health condition or disability changes, you should tell the DWP as soon as possible, either by phone or in writing. If you do this in writing, keep a copy of the letter for your records. If you phone, make sure you note the date and time of your call and keep a record of what was said.

The DWP reviews your PIP award to decide whether it needs to be adjusted to take account of your new circumstances. If it makes a new decision changing the amount of PIP you get, this is called a 'supersession'.

It is in your best interests to notify the DWP if your condition worsens, as this could mean you are entitled to a higher amount of PIP. The DWP can look again at your whole award, so there may be a risk to your current award as it could decide you are entitled to a lower award or no award at all. It could be useful to get medical evidence and/or seek advice *before* you tell the DWP that your condition has worsened.

Remember that you must report any change in your circumstances that might affect your entitlement, including if your condition improves. If you do not tell the DWP and it subsequently becomes aware of the change and adjusts your award at a later date, you may have been overpaid and may have to pay some money back. The DWP is aware that improvements can be gradual. It is all right to wait until significant improvements have happened before updating the DWP, and you should not be asked to pay back any PIP.

**What CPAG says**

**Changes of circumstances**

The rules say that you must tell the DWP of any changes that you are specifically asked to report, so check letters about your PIP award. You also have to report any other changes that you should know might affect your PIP, which could include if:

- the effect of your condition worsens
- the effect of your condition improves
- you stop receiving treatment
- you go into hospital or residential care
- you change your address or leave the UK
- you go into prison

If you are in any doubt about whether a change is relevant, you should seek advice.

If the DWP thinks you have been overpaid because you have deliberately not reported a relevant change in your circumstances, you may be considered to have acted fraudulently. This could lead to a criminal conviction or a financial penalty, and your PIP could be suspended for a set period. You should report immediately any change in your circumstances that might affect your entitlement. If you are not certain whether a change in your circumstances is relevant, you should report it. If you are accused of fraud or invited to an 'interview under caution', you should get specialist legal advice as soon as you can. It is worth noting that PIP fraud prosecutions are very rare.

In addition to the regular scheduled reviews of your PIP award, the DWP can also review your award if it believes that there may have been a relevant change in your circumstances.

As part of the review process, you must complete a new assessment questionnaire, and may have to attend another consultation. Try to provide as much evidence as possible of your current needs, such as a letter from your GP, hospital reports and medication details.

If you disagree with the decision following the review, you can ask for a mandatory reconsideration, and then appeal to a tribunal if necessary.

**EXAMPLE**

**Change of circumstances**

Amaiya has a degenerative eye condition. She already gets the standard rate of both the 'daily living component' and 'mobility component' of PIP. Her condition has got worse and she is now registered as severely sight impaired (blind). She calls the DWP and lets them know about the change. The DWP reassesses Amaiya and awards her the enhanced rates of the daily living and mobility components.

## *Further information*

CPAG produces another guide in this series called *Winning Your Benefit Appeal: what you need to know*.

CPAG's *Welfare Benefits Handbook* contains detailed information about challenging decisions and overpayments, with references to the legislation and caselaw.

# Chapter 8
# People in special circumstances

**This chapter covers:**

1. **Are you in hospital?**
2. **Are you in a care home?**
3. **Are you in prison?**

### What you need to know

- Both the 'daily living component' and the 'mobility component' of personal independence payment (PIP) can only be paid for a maximum of 28 days while you are in hospital or prison, unless you are under 18 when you go into hospital.
- The daily living component can only be paid for a maximum of 28 days while you are in a publicly funded care home. The mobility component is not affected.
- When calculating the 28-day time limit, different periods spent in hospital, prison or a care home can sometimes be linked.
- It is important to tell the DWP as soon as you have been in hospital, prison or a publicly funded care home for 28 days or you might be overpaid PIP and have to pay the money back.
- It is important to tell the DWP as soon as you leave hospital, prison or a publicly funded care home so that you can be paid PIP as soon as possible from the date you return home.
- If you claim PIP when you are in hospital, a care home or prison, you cannot be paid until you leave (unless you are under 18 and in hospital). If you are a publicly funded care home resident, this only applies to the daily living component.

## 1. Are you in hospital?

Your PIP is affected if you are a hospital inpatient, unless you went into hospital before your 18th birthday and have been there ever since.

If you were under 18 when you went into hospital, payment of your PIP continues throughout that stay as a hospital inpatient, even if you turn 18 during your stay. If you were under 18 when you went into hospital, you can claim PIP while you are in hospital.

If you are 18 or older and entitled to PIP when you go into hospital, your entitlement continues but payment stops after 28 days. The days you enter and leave hospital do not count. Payment can start again from the day you leave hospital.

If you are 18 or over when you go into hospital and are awarded PIP while you are in hospital, you cannot be paid until you leave.

Box A
**Are you a hospital patient?**

- A hospital can also include a 'similar institution' to a hospital. This is not defined in the regulations, but it could include a care home, clinic or rehabilitation unit where you are receiving NHS-funded treatment provided or supervised by qualified doctors, nurses or other 'healthcare professionals'.
- You do not count as being in a hospital if you are 'terminally ill' and in a hospice that is not an NHS hospital or similar institution.
- PIP is not affected if you are a private patient.

If the DWP has treated you as a hospital patient, but you think you should have been treated as being in a care home (in which case, payment of your 'mobility component' is unaffected), you should get advice. You may be able to challenge this decision.

Both the 'daily living component' and mobility component are affected if you are 18 or over and go into hospital.

If the DWP pays your mobility component directly to Motability to enable you to hire a car or wheelchair or buy one on hire purchase, payments will also stop after 28 days. You then have 28 days in which to return the car or wheelchair. This 28-day period may be extended by negotiation with Motability.

**EXAMPLE**

**Hospital and similar institution**

Jack is 42. He has been in hospital since late 2023. Jack is moved from a long-stay hospital into a nursing home where he receives medical treatment from staff based at the home. The NHS funds the treatment and the costs of his board and accommodation. Jack is entitled to both 'components' of PIP, but his payments stopped after he had been in hospital for 28 days. The DWP decides that Jack is now in a similar institution to a hospital and so his PIP is still not payable.

Theo had a stroke on 2 February 2024 and was taken to hospital. His PIP stopped after 28 days. He is transferred to a rehabilitation unit and expected to stay there for another six months. As the stay in the rehabilitation unit includes medical and nursing care provided by the NHS, Theo's PIP still cannot be paid.

### Have you had more than one stay in hospital?

Different periods spent as a patient that are separated by 28 days or less are linked together when working out whether you have been in hospital for 28 days, after which time your payment stops.

Periods you spend in a care home or prison also link with periods you spend in hospital, provided they are separated by 28 days or less. This means that if you have already been paid the daily living component of PIP for 28 days while in a care home and you go straight into hospital, you do not receive any further payment while in hospital if you are 18 or over. If you were getting the mobility component in the care home, it continues to be paid for the first 28 days you are a hospital patient.

EXAMPLES

**The linking rules**

Beatrice is 23. She is entitled to both components of PIP. She goes into hospital on 1 July for an operation and is discharged on 15 July. Her PIP is not affected because she has only been a patient for 13 days (the days she enters and leaves hospital do not count). On 30 July, she goes back into hospital for further treatment and is discharged again on 30 August.

There are 16 days between Beatrice's two hospital stays, so the days she spends in hospital are linked together. She has already received PIP for 13 days, so she can only be paid for a further 15 days, starting on 31 July. Her payments therefore stop from 15 August to 29 August.

Tariq is resident in a care home. His daily living component of PIP stopped after 28 days, but he still gets the mobility component. He goes into hospital for treatment. He cannot be paid the daily living component, but his mobility component continues to be paid for 28 days while he is in hospital.

### Have you been allowed home while you are in hospital?

If you have not been discharged from hospital officially but are allowed home for a few days, you can be paid PIP at the full amount for any nights that you are at home.

You will need to tell the DWP of the date that you go home and the date you return to hospital. You will need to send the DWP confirmation from the hospital of the dates you are at home.

## 2. Are you in a care home?

The 'daily living component' of PIP is affected if you are resident in a care home that provides nursing or personal care, and any of the costs of your accommodation, board and personal care are paid for out of public funds. As this applies to *any of the costs* being paid for out of public funds (usually by the local authority), your PIP is still affected if you pay a contribution towards your care, even if it is larger than the contribution the local authority pays. It does not apply if you fully fund the care yourself.

If you are entitled to the daily living component of PIP when you go into a care home, your entitlement continues, but payment stops after you have been resident for 28 days. The days you enter and leave the home do not count. Payment can start again from the day you leave the home.

If you are awarded the daily living component while you are resident in a care home, it cannot be paid until you leave.

The 'mobility component' of PIP is not affected if you are in a care home, regardless of how long you stay there.

You do not count as being in a care home, and therefore your PIP is unaffected, if you have a 'terminal illness' and you are in a hospice, provided this is not an NHS hospital or 'similar institution'.

You may not count as being in a care home if you are receiving a significant amount of nursing or medical care in the home; your placement is (or should be) partly funded by the NHS. In these circumstances, you count as being in a similar institution to a hospital and the above rules on hospital patients apply.

It is not always clear whether you are receiving public funding under the specified legislation or whether you are self-funding.

The DWP sometimes makes incorrect decisions based on inaccurate or unclear information provided by local authorities and care providers. If you think the DWP may have incorrectly stopped your daily living component, you should seek advice about challenging the decision. You can find sources of free advice using advicelocal.uk.

EXAMPLE

**Self-funding**

William is entitled to the daily living component of PIP. He is resident in a local authority care home.

The costs are fully paid by a combination of his benefits, a charitable payment and his brother. His daily living component remains payable because he is 'self-funding'.

Box B

**Paying for a care home**

- The daily living component of PIP only stops being paid if your accommodation, board and personal care are partly or wholly paid for by public funds under specified legislation. This does not include any benefits you may get. It does not matter whether it is a private or local authority care home – the important question is whether the local authority funds your place.
- If you are paying the full cost of your home and care yourself, or with the help of another person or a charity (ie. self-funding), you continue to be paid the daily living component. This also applies if a local authority is temporarily funding your placement while you sell your property, provided you are liable and able to repay the local authority when your property is sold (this is known as 'retrospective self-funding', but does not usually apply for the first 12 weeks you are permanently resident in a care home). The DWP may suspend payment of your daily living component while it makes enquiries about whether you are self-funding. Once this is established, payments should resume and arrears should be paid to you.

EXAMPLE

**Self-funding and local authority funding**

Hannah receives the daily living component of PIP when she permanently moves into a care home. She owns a property which she intends to sell. Her local authority ignores the value of the property for 12 weeks and fully funds her placement.

Her daily living component stops being paid after she has been resident in the home for 28 days.

After 12 weeks, she has still not sold her property. The local authority can no longer ignore its value, but agrees to continue funding until it is sold, on the basis that Hannah will repay the local authority when the property is sold. During this period, she counts as self-funding and the daily living component can be paid again.

Once the property is sold, Hannah continues to be self-funding until her savings fall below the level which entitles her to local authority funding again. When this happens, her daily living component will stop being paid.

## Have you had more than one stay in a care home?

Different stays in a care home separated by 28 days or less link together when working out whether you have been in a care home for 28 days, after which your daily living component stops.

Periods spent in prison or hospital (if you were 18 or over when you went into hospital) also link with periods spent in a care home, if they are separated by 28 days or less. This means that if you have already been paid the daily living component for 28 days while you were in hospital and you then go straight into a care home, you do not receive any further payment while you remain in the care home (unless you are self-funding). If you go in and out of residential care, you may want to plan the timing to maximise payment of your daily living component.

**EXAMPLES**

**Linking periods**

Helen is 64. She has been in hospital for several weeks and her daily living component of PIP has stopped being paid. She then moves permanently into a care home, paid for by her local authority. The daily living component is not payable because her stays in hospital and the care home are linked as they are separated by 28 days or less.

Tom spends periods in and out of residential care, funded by the local authority. He is entitled to the daily living component of PIP.

If Tom goes into a care home on Sunday and returns home the following Friday, he counts as being resident in the home for four days (the days he enters and leaves do not count). He can repeat this pattern for seven weeks before he counts as being resident in the home for 28 days, when his payments will stop.

If Tom goes home again, his payments will resume. If he spends at least 28 days at home, he continues to be paid for a further 28 days when he goes back into the care home.

## 3. Are you in prison?

Your PIP is affected if you are in prison or detained in legal custody.

If you are entitled to PIP when you enter prison, your entitlement continues, but payment stops after you have been in prison for 28 days. The days you enter prison and are released do not count. Payment can start again from the day you are released.

If you are awarded PIP while you are in prison, you cannot be paid while you remain in prison.

Both the 'daily living component' and 'mobility component' are affected if you are in prison.

Box C

**Are you in prison?**

- You do not count as being in prison or legal custody if you are on bail, or released on parole, temporary licence or under a home detention curfew (electronic tagging).
- You do not count as being in prison or legal custody if you are detained in a hospital or similar institution after criminal proceedings because of a mental disorder (but the hospital rules may apply), unless you have been detained under specified mental health legislation.

Different periods spent in prison that are separated by a year or less link together when calculating the 28-day period during which you can continue to get PIP while you are in prison. Periods spent in a care home or hospital (if you are 18 or over when you go into hospital) also link with periods spent in prison, provided they are separated by 28 days or less.

EXAMPLE

**Linking periods**

George is entitled to PIP when he is taken into legal custody. He continues to be paid for 28 days, after which it stops. A month later, he is released on bail and his PIP is paid again. Five months later, following a trial, he is imprisoned again. As this is within a year of his previous detention, payment of his PIP stops again the day after he goes to prison.

Chapter 9
# Personal independence payment and other benefits

This chapter covers:



## What you need to know

- If you get personal independence payment (PIP), you may be entitled to an extra amount in your 'means-tested benefits'.
- PIP does not affect your entitlement to most 'non-means-tested benefits'.
- Getting PIP means you are exempt from the 'benefit cap'.
- Your carer can claim carer's allowance if you get the 'daily living component' of PIP. This can affect your benefits though, so get advice first.
- If you get PIP, you may qualify for a 'Christmas bonus' and parking or travel concessions.
- If you get the enhanced rate 'mobility component', the Motability scheme can help you hire or buy a vehicle. You are also exempt from road tax (you get a 50 per cent reduction if you get the standard rate of the mobility component).

## 1. Means-tested benefits

'Means-tested benefits' are based on the amount of income and capital (such as savings) you have. They are:

- universal credit
- income support
- income-based jobseeker's allowance
- income-related employment and support allowance
- pension credit
- housing benefit
- child tax credit
- working tax credit

**Note:** you can now only make new claims for universal credit, pension credit and, in some very specific circumstances, housing benefit. The other benefits listed above are known as 'legacy benefits' and claimants of those benefits are being gradually moved to universal credit. The government aims to move most legacy benefit claimants to universal credit by the end of 2025.

PIP is not counted as income for means-tested benefits and therefore it does not reduce how much benefit you get.

### Can you get an extra amount?

If you get PIP, you may qualify for an extra amount in your means-tested benefit, such as a 'premium' in income support, income-based jobseeker's allowance, income-related employment and support allowance and housing benefit, an 'additional amount' in pension credit, or an 'element' in universal credit.

If you are entitled to any amount of PIP and are over pension age, you are automatically treated as having 'limited capability for work' for both employment and support allowance and universal credit.

If you are a full-time student and receive PIP, you may be able to claim universal credit when you could not otherwise. However, there are further complex conditions you would need to meet. Seek advice if you are in this situation.

Box A

**Premiums**

- If you are entitled to any amount of PIP, you qualify for a 'disability premium' in income support and income-based jobseeker's allowance. You qualify for a disability premium in housing benefit if you are under the qualifying age for pension credit (which is state pension age). There is no disability premium in employment and support allowance.
- If you are paid the enhanced rate 'daily living component', you qualify for an 'enhanced disability premium' in income support, income-based jobseeker's allowance, income-related employment and support allowance and housing benefit.
- If you are entitled to either rate of the daily living component, you may qualify for a 'severe disability premium' in income support, income-based jobseeker's allowance, income-related employment and support allowance and housing benefit, provided you meet other qualifying conditions.

Box B

**Universal credit elements**

- There is no equivalent to the severe disability premium in universal credit. If you are already getting the severe disability premium and move to universal credit, you might get a 'transitional severe disability premium element' in your universal credit.
- If you are entitled to the transitional severe disability premium element in your new universal credit award, you may also be awarded the 'transitional enhanced disability premium element', 'transitional disability premium element', 'transitional disabled child premium element' and 'transitional disabled child element'.
- If you are entitled to the enhanced rate daily living component and are over pension age, you qualify for a 'limited capability for work and work-related activity element' in your universal credit.

Box C
**Additional amounts**

- If you are entitled to either rate of the daily living component, you qualify for a 'severe disability additional amount' in your pension credit, provided you meet other qualifying conditions.

### Non-dependant deductions

If you or your partner are entitled to the daily living component of PIP, no 'non-dependant deductions' are made from any help with housing costs you might get through income support, income-based jobseeker's allowance, income-related employment and support allowance, housing benefit, pension credit or universal credit. A non-dependant deduction (known as a 'housing costs contribution' for universal credit) is an amount that is normally deducted from your means-tested benefit if you have an adult living with you who is not your partner. For universal credit only, no deduction is made from the housing costs of someone you live with due to your presence if you are entitled to the daily living component of PIP.

### Does your child get personal independence payment?

If you have a child who is 16 or over who receives PIP and still counts as part of your household, you qualify for:

- a 'disabled child premium' in your housing benefit; if they receive the enhanced rate daily living component of PIP, you also qualify for the 'enhanced disability premium'
- a lower 'disabled child addition' in your universal credit; a higher rate is paid if the child receives the enhanced rate daily living component of PIP

## 2. Other benefits

Other, 'non-means-tested', benefits are not affected by any income and capital you have.

PIP can be paid in addition to most non-means-tested benefits, such as:

- contribution-based jobseeker's allowance (called new-style jobseeker's allowance by the DWP)
- contributory employment and support allowance (called new-style employment and support allowance by the DWP)
- carer's allowance
- bereavement benefits
- child benefit
- statutory maternity, paternity and adoption pay
- statutory shared parental pay
- statutory sick pay
- maternity allowance
- retirement pension
- industrial injuries disablement benefit

Some non-means-tested benefits cannot be paid for the same person at the same time as PIP. These are:

- disability living allowance
- attendance allowance
- constant attendance allowance (this could be paid as part of your industrial injuries benefit or war pension, and 'overlaps' with the daily living component of PIP)
- war pensioners' mobility supplement payable under the War Pension Scheme, or grants for the use of a vehicle from the NHS (these 'overlap' with the mobility component)
- Scottish child disability payment
- Scottish adult disability payment
- Scottish pension age disability payment

## Carer's allowance

Carer's allowance is a benefit for people who provide care for 35 hours or more a week to someone who is sick or disabled and receiving a qualifying benefit. If you are entitled to either rate of the 'daily living component' of PIP and someone regularly cares for you, they can claim carer's allowance, provided they meet the other qualifying conditions. If your carer receives universal credit, they may also qualify for the carer 'element' of universal credit within their award. The carer does not have to receive carer's allowance to qualify for the carer element.

However, if you are entitled to a 'means-tested benefit' other than universal credit, you could lose money if someone claims carer's allowance or the carer element in universal credit for looking after you. This is because you may lose the 'severe disability premium' included in your benefit. The rules are complicated, so get advice before someone claims carer's allowance for looking after you.

## 3. The benefit cap

There is sometimes a limit on the total annual amount of benefits that you can receive if you are under pension age. This is known as the 'benefit cap'.

If you live outside Greater London the limits are:

- £1,229.42 a month (£283.71 a week) if you are single without children
- £1,835.00 a month (£423.46 a week) if you are in a couple or a lone parent

If you live within Greater London the limits are:

- £1,413.92 a month (£326.29 a week) if you are single without children
- £2,110.25 a month (£486.98 a week) if you are in a couple or a lone parent

If the total amount of certain benefits you receive is more than the limits above, your housing benefit or universal credit is reduced.

PIP is not one of the specified benefits included in the cap. If you, your partner or child get PIP, you are exempt from the benefit cap. This exemption still applies if you are entitled to PIP but it is not payable because you are in hospital or a care home. There are other exemptions too, so seek expert advice if you or your family are affected by the benefit cap.

Your carer will also be exempt from the benefit cap if they are entitled to carer's allowance or are getting universal credit that includes the carer element.

## 4. Other financial help

You may qualify for a 'Christmas bonus' if you are entitled to PIP. This bonus is currently £10.

If you have a low income, you may be entitled to a council tax reduction (sometimes called council tax support, discount or benefit). Contact your local authority for more information.

If you are entitled to the 'mobility component' of PIP, you may qualify for a blue badge for parking concessions. You may also qualify for a concessionary travel card. The rules are different in different areas. Contact your local authority for more information.

If you are entitled to the enhanced rate mobility component, you are exempt from road tax. If you are entitled to the standard rate mobility component, you can get a 50 per cent reduction in the cost of your road tax. Contact the Driver and Vehicle Licensing Agency (DVLA) for more information.

## 5. Motability

Motability is a scheme to help people with a long-term health condition or disability hire or buy a car, electric wheelchair or scooter. You can join the scheme if you receive the enhanced rate 'mobility component' and your award end date is 12 months or more away.

If you do not drive, but you receive the enhanced rate mobility component, you can apply for a car as a passenger, nominating a maximum of three other people as your drivers.

Under the scheme, your mobility component is paid directly to Motability as a payment towards a vehicle. You may also have to make extra payments to Motability. The vehicle can be adapted to suit your needs.

If your award of PIP ends, your entitlement to Motability ends and you would need to return any vehicle you were leasing. Special rules including a support package apply if you have been part of the Motability scheme since before the start of 2014 and are transitioning from disability living allowance to PIP but not awarded PIP. Contact Motability for more details.

## *Further information*

Contact your local Citizens Advice, local authority welfare rights service or other independent advice provider for more information about the benefits that you may qualify for if you are awarded PIP. Use advicelocal.uk to find a service near you. You can find further information about road tax at gov.uk/government/organisations/driver-and-vehicle-licensing-agency and about the Motability scheme at motability.co.uk (phone: 0300 456 4566; motability.co.uk/get-support/bsl-video-relay-service).

# Appendix 1

## Glossary of terms

**Activity/activities**
There are 12 'everyday activities' identified for personal independence payment (PIP). The PIP assessment looks at how your health condition or disability affects your ability to carry out these activities.

**Additional amount**
An extra amount of pension credit paid to people with additional needs, such as a disability or caring responsibilities.

**Appointee**
Someone, often a relative, authorised by the DWP to claim and receive benefit on another person's behalf if that person is either under 16 or cannot claim for themself – for example, because of a learning disability.

**Benefit cap**
The maximum amount of social security benefits that you can receive. The cap does not apply if you, your partner or a child still included in your benefit claim are entitled to child disability payment in Scotland, PIP or disability living allowance.

**Capital**
Includes savings, investments, certain lump-sum payments and property that is not your main home.

**Care component**
The part of disability living allowance paid if you need help looking after yourself or someone to keep an eye on you because of your disability or health problem.

**Case manager**
A member of staff employed by the DWP who makes decisions on entitlement to PIP, sometimes called a decision maker.

**Christmas bonus**
An extra payment of £10 paid to people receiving certain benefits (including PIP) in the week beginning on the first Monday in December.

**Component**
One of the two parts of a PIP or disability living allowance award.

**Daily living component**
The part of PIP paid if you have problems with daily living activities or are terminally ill.

**Decision notice**
The letter from the DWP that you receive with an initial decision, setting out how many points you scored for PIP and whether that means you will receive an award.

**Descriptor**
A statement describing your ability to carry out one of the specific daily living or mobility activities.

**Disability premium**
An extra amount of income support, income-based jobseeker's allowance and housing benefit paid to people getting PIP or certain other benefits, or who are registered blind.

**Disabled child addition**
An extra amount of universal credit paid for a child or young person who gets child disability payment in Scotland, disability living allowance or PIP, or who is registered blind.

**Disabled child premium**
An extra amount of housing benefit paid for a child or young person who gets child disability payment in Scotland, disability living allowance or PIP, or who is registered blind.

**Elements**
Amounts for children, disability, caring responsibilities, housing and childcare that make up part of someone's maximum universal credit award.

**Enhanced disability premium**
An extra amount of income support, income-based jobseeker's allowance, employment and support allowance and housing benefit paid to people getting the PIP enhanced daily living component, the disability living allowance high rate care component, the support component of employment and support allowance or, in Scotland, the highest rate of the care component of child disability payment.

**European Union Settlement Scheme**
A scheme to allow European Union citizens and their eligible family members who were living in the UK by 31 December 2020 to continue living in the UK.

**Habitually resident**
Someone who has a settled intention to stay in the UK, and who has usually been living here for a period.

**Healthcare professional**
A doctor, nurse, paramedic, physiotherapist or occupational therapist who carries out assessments for PIP.

**Housing costs contribution**
Deduction from your universal credit if certain other adults live with you.

**Limited capability for work element**
An extra amount of universal credit paid to people whose ability to work is limited because of illness or disability and who were assessed as having limited capability for work before 3 April 2017.

**Limited capability for work and work-related activity element**
An extra amount of universal credit paid to people who are too ill to look for work or who have a severe disability. Commonly known as LCWRA.

**Mandatory reconsideration**
When you ask for the DWP to change a decision on your benefit claim.

**Mandatory reconsideration notice**
Notice sent by the DWP after you make a mandatory reconsideration request that tells you whether or not the original decision has been changed, and is needed to appeal a decision.

**Means-tested benefit**
A benefit that is only paid if your income and capital are low enough, and which also considers the circumstances of your partner.

**Mobility component**
The part of PIP, disability living allowance, or child disability payment in Scotland paid if you have mobility problems.

**Non-dependant deductions**
Deductions from your housing benefit or universal credit if certain other adults live with you. In universal credit, non-dependant deductions are termed 'housing costs contributions'.

**Non-means-tested benefit**
A benefit that is paid regardless of the amount of your income or capital.

**Overpayment**
An amount of benefit that is paid to you, but which is more than your entitlement and which you may be asked to repay.

**Person subject to immigration control**
Someone who requires leave to enter or remain in the UK but does not have leave, or who has leave to remain but is prohibited from having recourse to public funds, or has leave to remain in the UK on the basis of a sponsorship agreement.

**Premium**
Extra amounts of benefit paid with means-tested benefits depending on your circumstances.

**Required period condition**
The qualifying period for PIP, normally three months before and nine months after the date of your claim.

**Retrospective self-funding**
A term used to describe when the local authority is temporarily funding your placement in a care home while you sell your property, after which you must repay the money.

**Revision**
A way that the DWP can change a benefit decision; it includes, but is not limited to, mandatory reconsiderations.

**Self-funding**
A term used to describe when you are paying the full cost of your placement in a care home yourself.

**Severe disability additional amount**
An extra amount of pension credit paid if you are getting the daily living component of PIP, attendance allowance or the disability living allowance middle or highest rate care component, and you satisfy certain other conditions.

**Severe disability premium**
An extra amount of means-tested benefits paid if you are getting child disability payment in Scotland, the daily living component of PIP, attendance allowance or the disability living allowance middle or highest rate care component and you satisfy certain other conditions. It does not exist in universal credit.

**Similar institution**
An institution that is similar to a hospital for the PIP rules.

**Supersession**
A term used by the DWP when it changes a benefit decision, usually as a result of a change in your circumstances.

**Terminal illness**
A progressive disease from which your death can reasonably be expected within 12 months.

**Transitional disability premium element**
An extra amount of universal credit paid to people entitled to the transitional severe disability premium element, who were entitled to the disability premium in their legacy benefit in the month immediately before universal credit started and continue to meet the criteria. Available from 14 February 2024 onwards.

**Transitional disabled child element**
An extra amount of universal credit paid to people entitled to the transitional severe disability premium element, who were entitled to the disabled child element in their tax credits in the month immediately before universal credit started and continue to meet the criteria. Available from 14 February 2024 onwards.

**Transitional disabled child premium element**
An extra amount of universal credit paid to people entitled to the transitional severe disability premium element, who were entitled to the disabled child premium in their legacy benefit in the month immediately before universal credit started and continue to meet the criteria. Available from 14 February 2024 onwards.

**Transitional enhanced disability premium element**
An extra amount of universal credit paid to people entitled to the transitional severe disability premium element, who were entitled to the enhanced disability premium in their legacy benefit in the month immediately before universal credit started and continue to meet the criteria. Available from 14 February 2024 onwards.

**Transitional severe disability premium element**
An extra amount of universal credit paid to people who were entitled to a severe disability premium in their legacy benefit in the month immediately before universal credit started and continue to meet the relevant criteria.

# Appendix 2

## Meaning of terms used in the descriptors

### Aided

With:

(a) the use of an aid or appliance; or

(b) supervision, prompting or assistance.

### Assistance

Physical intervention by another person; does not include speech.

### Assistance dog

A dog trained to guide or assist a person with a sensory impairment.

### Basic verbal information

Information in the claimant's native language conveyed verbally in a simple sentence.

### Basic written information

Signs, symbols and dates written or printed standard size text in the claimant's native language.

### Bathe

Includes getting into or out of an unadapted bath or shower.

### Communication support

Support from a person trained or experienced in communicating with people with specific communication needs, including interpreting verbal information into a non-verbal form and vice versa.

### Complex budgeting decisions

Decisions involving:

(a) calculating household and personal budgets;

(b) managing and paying bills; and

(c) planning future purchases.

### Complex verbal information

Information in the claimant's native language conveyed verbally in either more than one sentence or one complicated sentence.

**Complex written information**
More than one sentence of written or printed standard size text in the claimant's native language.

**Cook**
Heat food at or above waist height.

**Dress and undress**
Includes putting on and taking off socks and shoes.

**Engage socially**
(a) interact with others in a contextually and socially appropriate manner;
(b) understand body language; and
(c) establish relationships.

**Manage incontinence**
Manage involuntary evacuation of the bowel or bladder, including use a collecting device or self-catheterisation, and clean oneself afterwards.

**Manage medication**
Take medication, where a failure to do so is likely to result in a deterioration in the claimant's health.

**Manage therapy**
Undertake therapy, where a failure to do so is likely to result in a deterioration in the claimant's health.

**Medication**
Medication to be taken at home which is prescribed or recommended by a registered:
(a) doctor;
(b) nurse; or
(c) pharmacist.

**Monitor a health condition**
(a) detect significant changes in the claimant's health condition which are likely to lead to a deterioration in the claimant's health; and
(b) take action advised by a:
(i) registered doctor;
(ii) registered nurse; or
(iii) health professional who is regulated by the Health and Care Professions Council, without which the claimant's health is likely to deteriorate.

**Orientation aid**
A specialist aid designed to assist disabled people to follow a route safely.

**Prepare**
In the context of food, means make food ready for cooking or eating.

**Prompting**
Reminding, encouraging or explaining by another person.

**Psychological distress**
Distress related to an enduring mental health condition or an intellectual or cognitive impairment.

**Read**
Includes read signs, symbols and words but does not include read Braille.

**Simple budgeting decisions**
Decisions involving:
(a) calculating the cost of goods; and
(b) calculating change required after a purchase.

**Simple meal**
A cooked one-course meal for one using fresh ingredients.

**Social support**
Support from a person trained or experienced in assisting people to engage in social situations.

**Stand**
Stand upright with at least one biological foot on the ground.

**Supervision**
The continuous presence of another person for the purpose of ensuring the claimant's safety.

**Take nutrition**
(a) cut food into pieces, convey food and drink to one's mouth and chew and swallow food and drink; or
(b) take nutrition by using a therapeutic source.

**Therapeutic source**
Parenteral or enteral tube feeding, using a rate-limiting device such as a delivery system or feed pump.

**Therapy**
Therapy to be undertaken at home which is prescribed or recommended by a:
(a) registered:
(i) doctor;
(ii) nurse; or
(iii) pharmacist; or
(b) health professional regulated by the Health and Care Professions Council; but does not include taking or applying, or otherwise receiving or administering, medication (whether orally, topically or by any other means), or any action which, in the claimant's case, falls within the definition of 'monitor a health condition'.

**Toilet needs**
(a) getting on and off an unadapted toilet;
(b) evacuating the bladder and bowel; and
(c) cleaning oneself afterwards.

**Unaided**
Without:
(a) the use of an aid or appliance; or
(b) supervision, prompting or assistance.

*Schedule 1, Part 1 Social Security (Personal Independence Payment) Regulations 2013*

# Appendix 3

## Sources

### Personal independence payment legislation

Part 4 Welfare Reform Act 2012
The Personal Independence Payment (Transitional Provisions) Regulations 2013 No.387
The Social Security (Personal Independence Payment) Regulations 2013 No.377
The Personal Independence Payment (Supplementary Provisions and Consequential Amendments) Regulations 2013 No. 388
The Universal Credit, Personal Independence Payment, Jobseeker's Allowance and Employment and Support Allowance (Claims and Payments) Regulations 2013 No.380
The Universal Credit, Personal Independence Payment, Jobseeker's Allowance and Employment and Support Allowance (Decisions and Appeals) Regulations 2013 No. 381
You can find the legislation at legislation.gov.uk.

### Official guidance

Guidance for personal independence payment (PIP) decision makers at the DWP is in *Advice for Decision Making,* Chapters P1–6, available at gov.uk/government/publications/advice-for-decision-making-staff-guide.
Guidance for health professionals is in the *Personal Independence Payment Assessment Guide,* which is available at gov.uk/government/publications/personal-independence-payment-assessment-guide-for-assessment-providers.
There is also information about PIP for individuals and organisations in the *PIP Handbook* at gov.uk/government/publications/personal-independence-payment-fact-sheets/pip-handbook.

# Index